Kids' Bo

Kids' Book of Baseball

Hitting, Fielding, and the Rules of the Game

Godfrey Jordan

A Citadel Press Book
Published by Carol Publishing Group

For Thomas and Patrick

Carol Publishing Group Edition , 1995

Originally published as *The Official Kids' Book of Baseball*

A Citadel Press Book
Published by Carol Publishing Group
Citadel Press is a registered trademark of Carol Communications, Inc.
Editorial Offices: 600 Madison Avenue, New York, NY 10022
Sales & Distribution Offices: 120 Enterprise Avenue, Secaucus, NJ 07094
In Canada: Canadian Manda Group, One Atlantic Avenue, Suite 105
Toronto, Ontario, M6K3E7

Queries regarding rights and permissions should be addressed to:
Carol Publishing Group, 600 Madison Avenue, New York, NY 10022

Manufactured in the United States of America
10 9 8 7 6 5 4 3 2 1

Designer: Sharon Foster
Illustrations by: Stephen Quinlan and K. C. Rasmussen

Carol Publishing Group books are available at special discounts for bulk purchases, sales promotions, fund raising, or educational purposes. Special editions can also be created to specifications. For details contact: Special Sales Department, Carol Publishing Group, 120 Enterprise Ave., Secaucus, NJ 07094

Library of Congress Cataloging-in-Publication Data

Jordan, G. P. (Godfrey P.)
    Kids' book of baseball : hitting, fielding, and the rules of the
game / by Godfrey Jordan .
        p. cm.
    "A Citadel Press book. "
    ISBN 0-8065-1620-8 (pbk.)
    1. Baseball —Juvenile literature. [1. baseball.] I. Title.
GV867.5.J67   1995
796.357—dc20   94-45357
                                      CIP
                                      AC

Contents

INTRODUCTION

It's a great team sport with plenty of room for individual excellence. It requires just a few pieces of equipment — a ball, a bat and a glove. It can be played anywhere: an empty parking lot, a schoolyard, a country field. And anyone can have a chance to swing the bat and to catch the ball.

Sound like the perfect game? That's baseball!

And perhaps that's why baseball is played on every continent by more than 100 million people, in countries such as Japan, the Philippines, Russia, Egypt, Israel, Zimbabwe, Poland and Peru, to name just a few. It's also one of the fastest-growing sports in the People's Republic of China.

Baseball has been around for hundreds of years but is now more popular than ever. Attendance records are being set each year at Major League parks, and baseball became an official Olympic sport for the first time in 1992.

The Kids' Book of Baseball is jam-packed with tidbits about the history of the sport, useful tips on playing the game and oodles of fascinating trivia. Whether you want to learn how to play better or just see how the Major League pros make the game look so easy, the place to start is here.

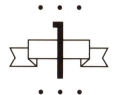

Ball + Bat + Glove = Baseball

All you need to play baseball is a ball, a bat and a glove. Let's take a look at these three basic pieces of equipment — and the "extras" that many teams use.

THE BALL

A baseball is specially manufactured to take a beating from bats and grounders, to bounce off fences and pound into mitts.

Rawlings manufactures all the regulation baseballs used in the Major Leagues. The parts are made in the United States and then shipped to Costa Rica for the final assembly and stitchwork.

A yarn is spun around a rubber and cork center. Holstein cowhide cut into a pattern with pre-stamped thread holes is then wrapped over top and sewn together tightly. The first and last stitch are tucked under the leather to leave no loose ends. An expert can stitch together a baseball with its distinctive 108 red stitches in just 10 minutes! The finished ball weighs between 5 and 5¼ ounces and measures between 9 and 9¼ inches in circumference.

And after all this, the baseball used in a professional league game will probably be replaced after only one hit! The players don't want to take the chance that the ball might not be perfect.

Balls used in softball games come in two sizes: the 7-ounce ball that is 12 inches in circumference and the 9- to 10-ounce ball that is 16 inches in circumference. These can be cowhide, nylon or rubber models that cover spun fibers.

One sporting goods company manufactures a special baseball designed to reduce injuries. The softer-on-impact RIF (Reduced Injury Factor) ball is not as hard as a regulation baseball, but it travels just as far when hit by a bat. Japanese youngsters have been playing with similar kinds of balls for years.

How Many Balls?

Each pro baseball team is supplied with about 12,000 balls for the season. League rules call for the umpires to be given 60 balls each game. And at least one dozen regulation balls are kept in reserve. Some baseballs go astray when fouled off into the stands, some are hit or scuffed, others are rejected by the pitcher for "not feeling right." The next time you watch a pro game, try to count the number of balls that pass through the pitcher's hands.

Ever wonder if the same ball could last for an entire nine-inning game? It happened on June 29, 1929, in a match between the Chicago Cubs and the Cincinnati Reds. No souvenirs for the fans in *that* game!

THE BAT

It's the bat that puts the ball into play and the numbers on the scoreboard.

Bats come in a variety of shapes and sizes and are made of wood or aluminum. A Major League bat must be wooden; most use the wood of the white ash tree.

The length and thickness of the bat can vary, but there are maximum restrictions. Though most players choose a bat between 34 and 37 inches long, a bat must be no longer than 42 inches, and the thickness at the hitting end can be no more than 2¾ inches.

A thick-handled bat allows for better control and is less likely to break. To provide extra grip, the handle is taped or covered with an adhesive solution such as pine tar. Most broken bats occur when thin-handled models connect on an inside pitch. The barrel end will splinter off and fly onto the field.

Aluminum bats are quite popular among non-professional teams and casual players. They cost more than wooden bats, but because they don't chip, dent or break easily, these metal bats last longer.

Deciding on the length and weight of a bat is a personal choice. If the bat lets you take an easy, even swing, that's the bat for you!

Find Your Bat's Sweet Spot

Each bat has its own "sweet spot." When a batter connects the bat's sweet spot to the ball, it knocks the ball the maximum distance for the swing.

To find your bat's sweet spot, hold your bat tightly by the handle, so that it is parallel to the ground. Ask a friend to drop a baseball onto the various places on the bat until you find the area that makes the ball bounce highest. With a felt pen, draw a small circle around this spot. The next time you step up to the plate, try to hit the ball on this section of the bat for your maximum hitting potential.

THE GLOVE

When the sport began, catching a ball with bare hands was the only way to play. But after too many bruises and fractured fingers, players began to wear a glove to protect their catching hand.

The glove (also called a mitt) is most often made from cowhide or leather, with nylon stitching. The four-fingered glove used by all fielders — except the catcher and the first baseman — has an enlarged enclosure for the thumb that is attached by leather straps. Because the catcher must stop pitches drilled in at speeds of 90 mph in the Major Leagues — and up to 60 mph in junior leagues — the catcher's glove is well padded and all in one piece, with a small opening between the thumb and the index finger.

The first baseman uses a "trapper." This glove is similar to the catcher's mitt but is flexible. The thumb of the glove is connected by leather webbing to the single piece containing the other four fingers.

Properly cared-for gloves can last for years. Loose stitching or a small rip in the seam can often be fixed in a shoe repair shop.

How to Make a Pocket

When you purchase a new glove, you're taking home a great-smelling, ultra-clean piece of sporting equipment.

But just as your body needs to get into shape before a game or workout, so too must your glove be properly broken in or "given a pocket." The pocket is the spot in the glove where you'll want to catch the ball.

Dampen the pocket with some hot water and then rub it with mineral oil, baby oil or saddle soap. Put the glove on and slap a ball into the pocket over and over again or ask a friend to play a hard game of catch.

You can also use twine or rope to tightly bind the ball within the enclosed glove, right where you'd like the pocket to form. Leave the glove in a place where it can dry for a day or two.

SUITING UP

A lightweight and durable baseball cap is an important part of your uniform. It can be easily tossed aside when you're running back to follow the path of a fly ball. But when it's on your head, the cap shades your eyes and protects them from harmful ultraviolet rays, and it can help prevent sunstroke.

Wear a batting helmet whenever you step up to the plate, during practice as well as in games. It protects your most valuable piece of baseball equipment — your brain. Most helmets are made of heavy-duty plastic and have an inner headband that can be adjusted for a snug fit. Some amateur leagues are using a batting helmet with a faceguard attached to it. This prevents many eye, cheekbone and dental injuries caused by wild pitches.

Unless they specify otherwise inside the headband, the plastic helmets bought as souvenirs from Major League parks are meant only for collecting and *NOT* for protection in the batter's box.

A variety of small, compact and padded batting

gloves are available to shield the hitter's hands from those high-speed inside pitches aimed at the spot where fingers grip the bat. Gloves ensure a secure grip.

Choose a shirt size large enough so you can wear an undershirt or long-sleeved sweater underneath on cool days or evenings.

Pants should be worn with a belt and be held in place just below the knee by a plastic strap. Make sure the pants aren't too baggy or too tight, but are comfortable to run and slide in. If your league permits sliding, you may want to wear sliding pads under the pants.

Everyday running shoes make fine baseball shoes. If your league requires the regulation leather-and-spike style worn by the pros, choose a pair that fit more snugly than your street shoes (loose shoes may cause ankle injuries). Keep them clean and dry them off thoroughly after playing on a wet day. Wearing a good pair of sweat socks is important; in some leagues, you may have to wear footless woollen stockings held in place by an elastic strap under the foot.

A jockstrap can be purchased at any sporting goods store and provides protection during falls, slides, collisions or grounders.

The catcher's mask, shin guards and body pads should fit you properly for maximum protection of your face, neck, shins, feet and chest. After each game or practice, dry out the guards and body pad thoroughly.

A padded vest worn by batters is now recommended for many young ballplayers to cover their upper body. It's the latest innovation for making baseball a safer sport.

THE FIELD OF DREAMS

This is where all the action happens! Take a look at the diagram of a regulation baseball field to see its layout and where the players, coaches and umpires are positioned.

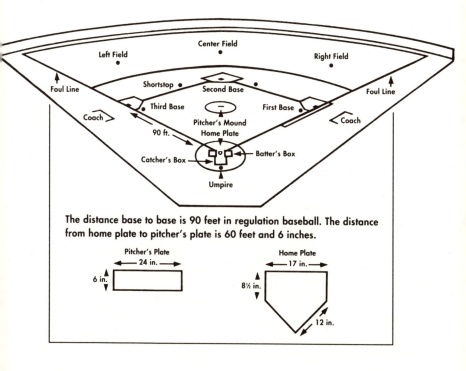

The distance base to base is 90 feet in regulation baseball. The distance from home plate to pitcher's plate is 60 feet and 6 inches.

The defensive team's nine players can be situated so that certain parts of the field are covered against an individual batter's style.

The offensive team has a coach at first base and at third base to advise the baserunners or signal to the batter.

Umpires are stationed near each base to keep order and settle any disputes. The umpire behind home plate calls the strikes and balls. The batter must remain in the batter's box while waiting for the pitch.

(Little League and most other junior games have the bases 60 feet apart; the pitcher-to-plate distance is 46 feet.)

Why is a left-handed person called a "southpaw"? In the early days of baseball, parks were laid out with home plate on the west side of the field. That meant a pitcher holding the ball in his left "paw" would be facing "south" and so he'd be a "southpaw"!

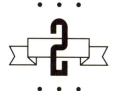

More Than One Way to Play

There are three variations of baseball: regulation baseball, softball and T-ball. They are very similar, but here's a brief description of each. Knowing the rules to a game makes it easier to learn the skills needed to play it — and it lets you help your team do its best by making as few errors as possible.

REGULATION BASEBALL

Regulation baseball is the popular Major League sport played by professionals. It is governed by the Official Playing Rules, adopted in 1904 and published by the Office of the Commissioner of Major League Baseball. As well as stating the rules about equipment, such as the maximum length of the bat, the weight of the ball and the dimensions of the playing field, the rule book has the final word for every situation that could possibly occur before, during or even after a game. Here are some of the key rules that will help you know what's fair or foul, what's a safe play and what's not.

A strike is:
- any swing of the bat that misses a pitch;
- any pitch thrown through the strike zone over home plate;
- any pitch that touches the batter as he swings at it;
- a foul tip, which goes directly off the bat into the catcher's glove;
- any hit (until the third strike) into foul territory. A ball hit into foul territory after the second strike is still called a foul ball but is not the third strike.

Three strikes make an "out." . . . Next batter up!

A ball is:
- a pitch thrown outside of the strike zone at which the batter doesn't swing.

Four balls and you're on first base!

A foul ball is:
- a batted ball that comes to a stop in foul territory without first landing fair beyond the bases;
- a short hit or bunt that rolls into foul territory before reaching the outfield;

- counted as a first or second strike against the batter. It is a third strike only if it is tipped foul and caught by the catcher before it touches the ground.

A batter is on base:
- if the hit is not caught before the first bounce and reaches fair territory and the batter reaches a base safely;
- if four balls are called by the umpire. This is called a "walk," or a "base-on-balls";
- if the catcher drops a third strike pitch and, under certain conditions, the batter reaches it safely (see p. 58);
- if a pitch outside the strike zone hits the batter despite his effort to get out of the way.

A batter is "out":
- if three strikes are called against him;
- if either foot is completely outside of the batter's box when he hits the ball;
- if he hits a foul or a fair ball that is caught by a fielder before it touches the ground;
- if an opposing player touches first base while holding the ball before the batter reaches the base;
- if he bunts foul on the third strike;
- if he makes contact with his own fair ball before a fielder touches it.

A baserunner may:

- step away from, or "lead off" from, his base and attempt to reach or "steal" the next base when the ball is in play.

(Some amateur leagues, however, allow no lead-offs or running until the ball is hit.)

A baserunner is "out":

- if touched with the ball when he's not on a base;
- if hit by a batted ball in fair territory before the ball has touched or passed an infielder;
- if he interferes with a fielder or runs three feet off the baseline to avoid being tagged;
- on a "force play." In this situation, the batter hits and the runner must advance a base to allow room for the baserunner coming behind him. The fielder in possession of the ball has to touch that open base before the first runner reaches it.

Play stops and the ball is "dead":

- if a batter hits a foul that is not caught in the air;
- if a batter is hit by the ball;
- if the umpire asks for a time-out;
- if the umpire wants to examine the baseball;
- if a manager is given a time-out to change the players' position on the field or to make a substitution;
- if, during a play, a fielder falls into the dugout or spectator stands;
- if the ball leaves the playing field and is not a home run.

A player scores a run:
- when he legally touches first, second, third base and then home plate.

A game is over:
- after nine complete innings of play. However, the game can end before nine complete innings are played if the home team is already leading in runs at the middle of the ninth inning; the game ends without the home team needing to bat again;
- if the score is tied after nine complete innings, "extra" full innings will be played until the tie is broken;
- if it is stopped by the umpire, because of bad weather or other circumstances, after five full innings that make it a "complete" game with the scoring standing. (If five full innings have not been played, the game does not count and could be replayed entirely at another time.)

Writing Down the Rules

If you looked back over hundreds of years, you'd probably see many games that were quite similar to baseball. From the British "stoolball" of the 1200s, rounders, cricket and "one old cat" of the 1700s, running around bases while chased by a ball has been a popular pastime.

In 1838 baseball's first recorded game was played in Canada, in the village of Beachville, Ontario, near Toronto. That June 4 game involved the Beachville club and the Zorras, a team from a nearby township.

Who "invented" modern baseball?

Was it Abner Doubleday? The story goes that in 1839 in Cooperstown, New York (now home of the Baseball Hall of Fame), he sketched out a field and organized a game with cadets from a nearby military school.

Or was it Alexander Cartwright, a surveyor and fireman from New York City? In 1845, Cartwright formally wrote down the rules to a game he and his friends had been playing on summer fields. For the first time, such specifics as the size of the ball, the distance between the pitcher's mound and home plate, how many strikes would make an out and how many outs would make an inning were established.

SOFTBALL

The playing area of a softball game is smaller than that of a regulation baseball game. The distance from pitcher's mound to home plate is 46 feet for men's games and 40 feet for women's and youngsters' games, and the distance between bases is 60 feet. The ball used in softball is not any "softer" than a regulation baseball, but it is pitched with an underarm throw.

Softball is divided into two types of play: fast pitch and the more easy-going slow pitch.

Fast Pitch

The rules of fast-pitch softball allow the pitcher to rocket the ball underarm across the plate with no limit to speed. Some fast-pitch balls may reach up to 90 mph, the same speed as a Major League pitch.

Slow Pitch

The purpose of a slow-pitch game is to give everyone a chance to hit the ball, so rules limit the speed of the ball and the umpire determines if the pitcher is throwing too fast. A slower pitch results in more hits for the batter and more opportunities for the fielders to catch and throw.

In addition, most junior school and slow-pitch games have the following rule variations:
- a game is seven innings, instead of nine;
- a runner is not allowed to lead off from a base until the pitch has crossed home plate;
- a batter is not allowed to run if the catcher drops the third strike pitch;
- a runner is allowed to take only one extra base following a wild throw.

The Origin of Softball

Softball, or "indoor baseball" as it was originally known, was played for the first time in Chicago in the 1880s. A group of people had gathered in a small building to wait out a bad storm. Bored by the delay, a man tied up a boxing glove with a lace string and then tossed it, underarm-style, to a friend holding a broomstick. When that person swung at the "ball," the game of softball was born!

Around 1900, the game was modified by military men looking for some fun. The game was played inside huge armories by teams with eight players on each side, and foul balls were not counted as strikes. The ball used was a larger, softer version of the outdoor variety — and thus took on the name "softball." When the game eventually moved outside, softball rapidly gained popularity. Softball leagues formed and organized their own national association.

T-BALL

This game is the best news for kids under nine years old who are not yet ready to play softball or regulation baseball. Because there is no pitcher and the ball is hit off a tee above home plate, the batter has a perfect opportunity to put the ball into play.

T-ball has some rules that differ from regulation baseball. Depending on the players' age and skill, T-ball rules may vary from league to league. Check with your local organization.

- the pitcher does not throw the ball but is positioned as an infielder;
- a special foul area extends in a semicircle eight feet outward from home plate. Hits that land inside this area are dead balls;
- there are no "balls" or "walks" in T-ball. There are only hits or strikes. A player has only three chances to

hit the ball off the tee. Three swings that miss the ball (fanning the air or knocking the pole) and the batter is "out";

- the hitting team is "out" after every person on the team has come to bat in the inning. This gives the other team a chance to hit without having to stand out in the pasture all day! Everybody gets an equal chance to join in the fun.

In recreational leagues, the game might be the same, but the rules can vary. Check with your local baseball association for their list of "what's fair, what's foul" so that your team can play the best game possible.

Back to the Basics

Every physical action in baseball can be reduced to four basic skills: throwing, catching, hitting and running. That's why it is important to do them properly from the beginning. Any player — amateur or professional — can benefit from a review of these skills. All it takes then is practice, practice, practice!

WARM-UP EXERCISES

Think of all the running, jumping and throwing involved in a game of baseball — and all those lightning-fast twists and turns required to make the big plays! Doing a good series of warm-up exercises will get you limbered up for baseball practice or a game and will help keep you injury-free.

Include exercises to loosen and stretch muscles, such as rotating your ankles and wrist, and touching your toes with alternating hands; bent-knee sit-ups and push-ups to increase your upper-body strength as well as your hand and arm stamina; jumping jacks for an overall coordination of movement; and an easy jog around the park for the final loosening-up of muscies.

THROWING

"You spend a lot of time throwing a baseball, and in the end it turns out that it was the other way around all the time!" — with apologies to Jim Bouton, pitcher

The Standard Grip

Hold the ball in your hand with your "target fingers" (the index finger and the middle finger) in a V with a space the width of your index finger between them.

Position the ball so that your target fingers point in the direction of the seams on the ball or cross over them.

Curl your thumb underneath to support the ball, and bend in your little finger and ring finger to help center the ball in your grip.

Treat the ball as if it is a soft, ripe tomato. Hold it firmly, but don't squeeze it.

The Throwing Motion

Turn your body sideways, with your glove-hand side to the target. Draw your ball-hand back, with your elbow bent, and let your weight shift onto your rear leg. This will cause your hips to rotate slightly.

Now, keeping your wrist steady and angled forward, reverse these motions. Point your front foot directly toward the target to direct your throw. As you transfer your weight from your rear leg to your other leg, your hips will rotate back toward the target.

Moving your arm overhead causes the wrist to snap naturally. Release the ball just past and above your head.

Follow through. Let your arm continue its downward motion and your body shift in the direction of the ball to give your throw speed and accuracy.

Practice throwing to a partner, concentrating on your technique and the accuracy of your throw. If you can find a used car tire, suspend it with strong rope from a tree branch about six to eight feet above the ground and practice throwing balls through the hole. As you improve, give yourself the added challenge of a moving target by swinging the tire back and forth.

CATCHING

"Catching a flyball is a pleasure; knowing what to do once you catch it is business." — Tommy Henrich, New York Yankees

The Two-Handed Catch

Using the two-handed catching technique helps get the ball in your glove — and keeps it there!

Aim the pocket of your glove at the ball; bring your other hand up behind the glove to support and hold it steady. When the ball hits the glove, clutch your fingers together to trap the ball.

The Pop-Fly

Always face a pop-fly to catch it. If the ball is hit over your head, you'll have to "catch on the fly." Don't run backward, but keep your eye on the ball as you move quickly to where the ball is coming. Then turn around into the ball and raise your hands for a two-handed catch.

As you look up at the ball, raise your glove above your head, up and in front of your face, without blocking the ball from your eyes. Steady the glove from behind with your other hand. With your arms up and extended, you have a chance to recover the ball if it drops out of the pocket.

Practice catching pop-flys by having a friend with a tennis racquet drop-hit tennis balls high into the air toward you. After some stationary catches, have your friend hit the ball farther so you can practice "catching on the fly."

Or get a few friends and find a high, windowless wall. Throw a rubber ball so that it hits the ground in front of the wall and bounces up to hit the wall and then loops back in the air, creating low pop-ups and longer, floating flyballs. Concentrate on using the proper technique to catch the ball. Take turns catching and throwing the ball. Why not make a game of this by keeping score of all the catches made by each person?

The Grounder

Stopping a sharply hit ground ball is a standard play for infielders; outfielders have to worry about the bounces such a ball takes before it gets to them.

Never take your eyes off the path of a grounder. Move so that the ball comes directly toward you. Then "drop the curtain." This means getting into a crouched position, leaning forward as if on a racing bicycle and at the same time lowering the tip of your glove so it touches the ground. This way you can easily pull your glove up to catch the ball that bounces, and if the ball misses your glove it will likely be blocked by your body.

Keep your bare hand open, right beside the pocket, and use it as a backup to snag any ball that starts to come loose or to quickly pull the ball out of the glove for the follow-up throw to a base.

★ PRACTICE TIPS ★

Throw a rubber ball low against a windowless wall so that it bounces back hard against the ground toward you. Practice "dropping the curtain," snapping up the ball, using your bare hand to trap it and throwing it back at the wall.

Or take a position inside the infield and have a friend stand at home plate who throws the ball on the ground so that it takes one or two bounces. Move into position, recover it properly and throw the ball back to home plate, as if you are trying to get a baserunner out.

PITCHING

"Hitting is timing. Good pitching disrupts timing."
— Warren Spahn, Hall of Fame pitcher

Pitching is the art of controlled high-speed throwing. The pitcher must direct the ball into a space above home plate and between the batter's knees and armpits to get the batter swinging. The trick to successful pitching is to feed the ball through those edges of the strike zone where a batter has difficulty hitting.

Pitching requires a precise set of skills: the starting position, the delivery and the pitch. Your starting position and delivery should be regular and consistent, no matter what kind of pitch is to be thrown. Keep the batter guessing!

THE WIND-UP

The Starting Position

The starting position should loosen up your arm and shoulder muscles and make it easier for you to shift your balance.

There is a choice of two starting positions: the wind-up and the set position.

Wind-up

The full wind-up allows the maximum transfer of energy to go into a pitch, through body movement.

AND DELIVERY

Stand facing the batter. Your pivot foot (left for the left-handed pitcher, right for the right-handed pitcher) must be touching the pitcher's plate, but your other "free foot" may take one step backward and one step forward when you pitch.

Set Position

This half wind-up is ideal to control a baserunnner who might be threatening to steal a base. In the set position, your pivot foot returns to the rubber as you face the batter and hold the ball in both hands. Here you must come to a complete stop. You can either quickly throw for a pick-off play to any occupied base or continue the pitch to the batter.

It keeps the runner — and the batter — guessing.

If you choose the pick-off play, you must take a step toward that base or you'll be charged with a "balk."

The Delivery

Try for a smooth, even delivery with a rolling shoulder motion as your weight shifts from back leg to front leg to power the ball. You can "deliver" the ball overhand, side-arm or in between these at a three-quarters position.

A consistent delivery that doesn't vary with different types of pitches keeps the batter uncertain of what to expect.

The Follow-through

When the pitch is complete, your foot on the glove side should point directly at home plate. Stand on the mound facing the batter and be ready to stop any possible hit.

The Pitches

An effective hurler is able to control four main pitches: the fastball, the change-up, the curve and the slider. The first two are described here.

Fastball

This is the only pitch necessary for young pitchers to learn. It is the fastest ball that can be thrown from the mound. There's nothing fancy about it — no dips or doodles as it reaches home plate. The sole purpose of the fastball is to drill it by the batter as quickly as possible. Your speed won't match that of the great Nolan Ryan, who has been clocked throwing at more than 100 mph! But a controlled and accurate fastball will give any pitcher the edge on hitters.

Review the standard grip (see p. 28), making sure the tips of your index and middle fingers touch the ball across the seams. Then add your starting position and delivery. Release the ball, letting it roll straight off the ends of your fingers.

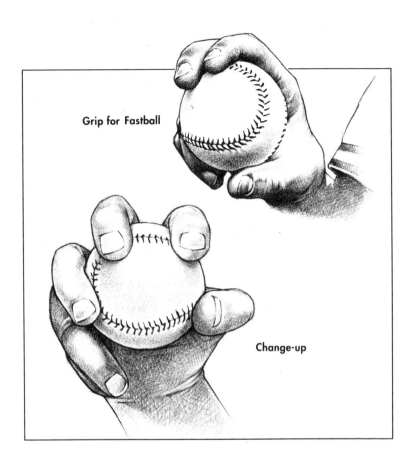

Grip for Fastball

Change-up

Change-up

When the batter senses that every ball thrown from the mound reaches the plate at the same speed, he can time his swing to better meet the next pitch. The change-up takes the batter off guard. Readied in a crouch to meet a 90-mph fastball, he may lose his concentration when the slower change-up pitch reaches the plate.

Hold the ball with the standard grip, and let the ball settle back in the palm of your hand. Let your thumb steady it there. Keep your wrist tight as you deliver and release the ball.

Softball Pitching

Pitching a fast pitch softball requires many of the techniques found in regulation baseball. The grip is similar, but holding a regulation baseball is like gripping a small apple, while holding a fast pitch softball is like gripping a grapefruit.

The fastball and curveball are the two most popular pitches in the game. Gripping across or along the seams on the ball — with the correct wrist action — controls the pitch.

One of the most familiar softball pitching styles is the "windmill." The wind-up motion resembles a windmill in action. Stand on the rubber facing the batter. Begin to transfer your weight forward onto your front leg as you move your glove hand and pitching arm forward in an underhand motion.

Your glove hand remains in front of your body as your pitching arm continues to move, rising above your head and around until it becomes a fully circular motion. Release the ball as the underarm motion gains its maximum speed, about the time that your pitching hand is alongside your hip. Let the follow-through bring you into a forward hop off the rubber. Remain alert and ready to field a hit.

Find an old carpet and paint the strike zone area on it. (The height from your knees to your mid-chest and 17 inches across.)

Hang the carpet against a fence or wall, and use a stick to mark a pitching mound (40 feet away for softball, 46 feet away for Little League, 60 feet away for regulation baseball). Pitching at the carpet target allows you to concentrate on your starting position, delivery, pitch and follow-through.

You can also use chalk to draw a strike zone on a windowless wall. Divide the strike zone into quarters. Get a rubber ball that is the size of a regulation baseball (the popular red-and-blue ball with a white stripe around the middle is perfect — you can use the stripe as a guide to the seams) and pitch to each of the four chalked boxes within the strike zone. Target the low areas of the strike zone for most of your throws.

Build a sequence so that you can throw high outside, low inside, low outside, high inside, and keep repeating it.

HITTING

"Good hitters are made, not born." — Ted Williams, the last player to bat over .400 in a season

Hitting a pitched baseball is an amazing athletic feat. If a fastball leaves the pitcher's hand at 95 mph to travel 60 feet toward home plate, the batter has less than half a second to decide whether to swing the bat. That's why one of the most important things you must practice as a hitter is keeping your eye on the ball from the moment the pitcher goes into his starting position. The rest is pure mechanics: the grip, the stance and the swing.

The Grip

Hold the bat. If you're left-handed, you'll put your left hand above your right; if you're right-handed, you'll put your right hand above your left. Close your grip so that the tops of your knuckles of both hands line up.

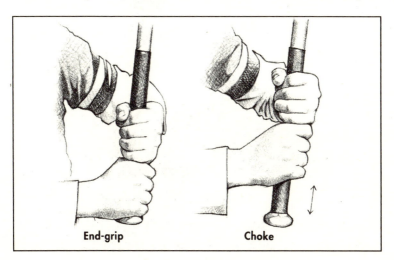

End-grip   Choke

Where you grip the bat is a matter of choice and will limit the kind of hit you can make.

The end-grip gives you the maximum use of your bat's big-hit potential.

The mid-grip is the best all-purpose grip, giving both good hitting power and good bat control.

The choke won't give you a home run, but you will have total bat control and be able to choose the direction of your hit more precisely.

The Stance

Step into the middle of the batter's box and face home plate with the side of your body toward the pitcher's mound. Point your forward foot, the one closest to the pitcher, toward the middle of home plate. Keep the other foot a shoulder-width away and parallel. Bend your knees slightly, to give yourself some bounce, and remain relaxed and flexible. Hold your arms out from your body with the bat handle in front of your back shoulder and the tip of the bat up and behind your back shoulder. You may wish to take a practice swing to make sure the barrel end of your bat reaches the space across the far end of the plate — and all the other areas of the strike zone.

The Swing

The ideal swing forms a perfect arc, from the top of the backswing to the end of the follow-through. Aim to contact the ball with the bat out in front of your body, as the ball enters the strike zone.

Timing the swing is crucial. As the pitcher releases the ball, have your weight on your rear leg. Raise your front foot slightly and quickly decide whether this is the pitch to hit. If it is, step into the hit, your outstretched arms bringing the bat across the plate as your body weight shifts from your back foot to the front foot. Your front foot lands on the ground with all your weight a split second before the bat and ball connect.

Follow through on the swing. Let your wrists roll as the bat comes around to your other shoulder.

Find a ball of wool or yarn that is the size of a baseball, and hang it outdoors from a tree branch (or, if there's plenty of room to safely swing the bat indoors, from a ceiling hook).

Practice your swing, concentrating on your hitting style. Occasionally adjust the height of the ball and your distance from it so that you practice hitting to every area in your strike zone.

The Bunt

The best bunt is an unexpected one. It's the hitter's version of a change-up. A surprise bunt can confuse the fielders who have been prepared to respond to a full hit.

The Grip

Because the bunt is a surprise move, begin with your standard bat grip but then move your hands to the bunt grip as the pitcher is delivering the ball. Grip near the tip of the handle with one hand and slide the other hand up to the mid-point of the bat. Keep a loose grip with your fingers tucked in behind.

The Stance
Begin with your regular stance. Then, as the pitcher starts to deliver the ball, step back with your front foot and bring your rear foot around so that you are facing the pitcher. Shift to the bunt grip and lift the bat into a horizontal position in front of home plate.

The Move
Don't punch the bat at the ball. Use the bat to "trap" the ball and guide it downward toward a baseline.

★ PRACTICE TIPS ★

Practice shifting into the bunt position, imagining that you've become like a door, opening and closing.

Have a friend stand about 10 feet away and lob underhand balls toward the strike zone. Practice bunting until you can easily guide each ball downward. Then have your friend pitch from the mound and repeat the technique.

RUNNING

"The only thing running and exercise can do for you is make you healthy." — Denny McLain, Detroit Tigers pitcher

Hitting and running are the two ways to score in baseball. Every hitter wants to get on base — and then become a runner. The moment you hit the ball, you become a "sprinter." Take short, powerful steps, lean forward, run on the front of your feet and keep your arms in tight and pumping.

Run a few feet to the right of the baseline, just inside of foul territory. This will prevent any interference with a fielding play and prepare you for a quick turn toward second base.

When you hit, race directly at first base and step on it in a motion that takes you farther down the baseline. Then turn right, into foul territory. You can over-run first base safely, but if a fielder has to recover a ball dropped on the throw to first, you can't be tagged out if you're in foul territory.

When you hit the ball and the coach waves you on, you must make a tight turn at first base. Timing your step so that one foot touches the inside part of the base (closest to the pitcher's mound) will help you to trim the looping distance you need to run on to second.

"Hug the basepaths" by running as close as possible to the middle zone between the bases. The shortest distance between two points is a straight line — and with a well hit ball, your reflexes and a fast pair of legs make that distance even shorter.

And always "hustle" — you'll boost the spirit of your whole team!

Sliding

"Sliding head-first is quicker — and it gets your picture in the paper." — Pete Rose

Sliding into a base does more than stir up the dust: it can give a runner a big advantage during a game. By coming in fast and low on a base, you are more difficult to tag and there's a chance your move could knock the ball loose from the fielder's glove. It can also prevent you from over-running a base. And in all the commotion, the baseman trying to stop you might miss the tag completely.

The head-first slide might be popular with the pros, but it is dangerous and not recommended for young players. Instead, go feet first. Think of the basepath as a long chute you are going to slide along. Run quickly toward the base and, about eight feet from the target, turn your body slightly to the side and drop into a sitting position. Keep your upper leg straight and pointing toward the base. Bend the leg that is underneath and slide on your calf. Keep your hands up so they won't get hurt. If you go with the motion, the slide will carry you right into the base.

★ PRACTICE TIPS ★

Practice sliding before trying it in a game. Wear long, loose-fitting trousers or sweat pants, a long- sleeved sweatshirt and running shoes.

Don't practice sliding on the diamond right away; the soil is probably stony and hard. Practice in the long grass in the outfield, in a sandy longjump pit or on a sandy beach — where you can go swimming after sliding!

You might also be able to practice indoors using your school's wrestling mats. Connect several together and use them as a padded landing zone with an old cushion or a base as your target.

"TAKE ME OUT TO THE BALL GAME"

Take me out to the ball game,
Take me out to the crowd.
Buy me some peanuts and Cracker Jack.
I don't care if I never get back
Let me root, root, root
For the home team.
If they don't win it's a shame
For it's one!
Two!
Three strikes — you're out!
At the old ball game!

© 1908 by Jack Norworth

DID YOU KNOW?

- Every ballpark has its bleachers. They are the seats without any back supports that are mostly located beyond the outfield fences. It's the place where the fans get "to bleach" in the direct sunlight!
- "Bleacher creatures" is the name given to the rowdy, boisterous fans who inhabit the bleachers.
- The "seventh inning stretch" takes place before the home team comes to bat in the seventh inning. All the fans stand

up and — you guessed it! — s-t-r-e-t-c-h. There are many stories to explain how this odd ritual came to be. A favorite one points to a day in 1910 when American president William Howard Taft was at a baseball game. He happened to stand in the middle of the seventh inning and so, out of politeness, all the fans stood up. Another report says that the custom was popular during the 1890s, with the superstitions about "lucky number 7" meant to bring good luck to the home team. Have you heard any other explanations?

- The word "fan" comes from the word "fanatic." The term was first used in 1884 by Chris Vonderahe, owner of the St. Louis Browns, to describe the wild enthusiasm of his audience.

- Artificial turf first appeared in the Houston Astrodome in 1966 and became known as Astroturf. It never has to be cut or watered. Ten Major League parks have artificial turf; the other sixteen parks continue to mow their lawns. Players agree that artificial turf does change the game of baseball. Balls hit on turf bounce faster and higher. A soft bunt cushioned to a stop on grass becomes a rolling ball if it lands the same way on artificial turf. And because most turf is rolled over concrete surfaces, the only cushion provided is the spongy rubber underpadding. Fielders who slip on Astroturf can get "carpet-burns," or skin irritations, from rubbing against the turf.

What a Position to Be In!

Almost every player on a baseball team must have the same basic skills: throwing, catching, hitting and running. Only the pitchers in the American League are not required to hit. A designated hitter takes their place in the batting order. That way, the pitcher only has to concentrate on pitching, and the designated hitter only has to concentrate on being a great hitter. The fans love it!

The other players must be able to hit well and play a position on the field when their team is on the defensive. Each position demands specific skills and strategies. It takes athletic skills, lots of practice and quick thinking to play a position well.

Let's look at the strategies of the offensive positions — the hitter and the baserunner — and then the defensive positions.

THE HITTER

One of the key things a batter must remember is to always run after hitting the ball. That high blooper you just hit toward their all-star shortstop could be fumbled — and if you don't run, you'll be left standing in the batter's box as the ball is tossed over to first. Bad for your batting average, bad for your image.

There is a standard way to hit a baseball (see "Hitting" in the previous chapter), but many hitters have developed their own style. Each style of swing affects where the ball goes and how far it travels. Here are four common styles of hitting.

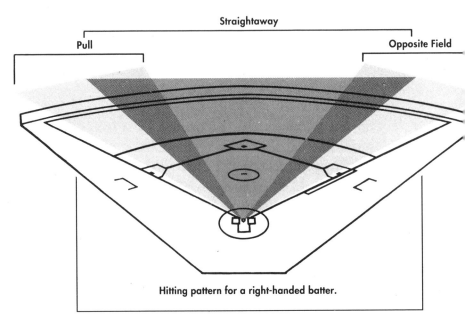

Hitting pattern for a right-handed batter.

The Pull Hitter
- hits to the same side of the field as the side of the plate the batter stands on: a left-handed batter "pulls" the ball in to the right side of the field and a right-handed batter "pulls" it to the left side of the field;
- connects with the ball before it passes over the plate;
- can hit with a lot of power.

The Straightaway or Spray Hitter
- hits the ball to match the pitch: he "pulls" an inside pitch to his side of the field; he hits an outside pitch to the field he is facing; he drives a center-plate pitch toward center field.

The Choke Hitter
- grips the bat high up on the handle and gets maximum bat control from the shorter swing;
- can easily hit anywhere he wants around the diamond;
- gets lots of single-base hits.

The Opposite Field or Late Hitter
- slices the ball into the opposite side of the field from the side of the plate he stands on: a left-handed batter hits toward third base and a right-handed batter hits toward first base.

The Batting Order

The manager knows each hitter's strengths and weaknesses. The batters must hit in the same order throughout the game. Before a game starts, the team manager gives the home plate umpire their starting line-up. No changes or substitutions can be made, unless the umpire has been notified. A player who substitutes for another batter is known as a "pinch hitter." The player who has been replaced cannot come back into the game.

The manager tries to create a batting order — putting certain players to bat before or after other hitters — that will use each player's skills to the best advantage. It takes science, savvy and baseball instinct to do it right. For example, here's a batting order arranged by Toronto Blue Jays manager Cito Gaston.

TORONTO BLUE JAYS BATTING ORDER
1993 WORLD SERIES GAME #1

1. Rickey Henderson (left field)
2. Devon White (center field)
3. Roberto Alomar (second base)
4. Joe Carter (right field)
5. John Olerud (first base)
6. Paul Molitor (designated hitter)
7. Tony Fernandez (shortstop)
8. Ed Sprague (third base)
9. Pat Borders (catcher)

Usually the best hitters are placed in the first five positions of the order, where they are likely to get the most at-bats during a game. However, this particular line-up featured so much hitting talent (including the year's top three American League Batting Champs) that Cito Gaston had to make choices that most managers only dream about.

Let's use the Blue Jays' 1993 statistics to demonstrate the batting order theory.

BATTER #1 — The lead-off hitter must get to first base a lot and use his running skills to steal second. (Rickey Henderson is baseball's all-time leader of stolen bases with 1,095; in 1993 he stole 53 bases and received 120 walks.)

BATTER #2 — Another reliable batter who can find his way to first base and move the lead-off man with well-directed hits. (Devon White is a switch hitter who stole 34 bases, got 163 hits — 42 of them doubles — and walked 57 times.)

BATTER #3 — The third batter must be a good RBI (runs-batted-in) man with power to hit the big one. (Another switch hitter, Robbie Alomar got 93 RBIs, hit .326, reached base safely in 30 consecutive games to set a Jays team record and stole 55 bases.)

BATTER #4 — The "clean-up" position requires a power hitter, capable of driving in a baserunner during critical situations such as two-out in an inning. (Joe Carter led the team again with most RBIs (121) and 33 homers. Of course, winning the World Series with a bottom-of-the-9th blast made his "clean-up" role complete.)

BATTER #5 — The third "tower of power" must follow up on any leftovers from the previous hitters. (John Olerud led the American League in 3 categories: batting (.363 average), the most doubles (54) and the highest On-Base Percentage (.473) He also had 107 RBIs.)

BATTER #6 — After the storm, this calm and steady hitter should be able to place hits carefully and get his bases aggressively. (Paul Molitor led the American League for most hits (211), and placed second for runs (121). His batting average of .332 put him second in the AL standings behind teammate Olerud.)

BATTERS #7 and #8 — These players are invited to get on base in any manner. (Tony Fernandez left a hitting slump behind in June after being traded from the N.Y. Mets and ended the season with a .306 average. Third baseman Ed Sprague got an impressive 142 hits and batted .260.)

BATTER #9 — This batter is generally the most unpredictable hitter on the team. In the National League, the pitcher usually comes to bat here, and is likely to bunt. That means those players in the seventh and eighth position who may be on base had better be good runners. (Pat Borders made this spot look good by getting 124 hits, including 30 doubles, for a .254 average.)

THE BASERUNNER

Running quickly and sliding well are important skills for the baserunner. A good baserunner remains alert to take advantage of opportunities to "steal a base," or reach a base without waiting for the ball to be hit. Major League rules allow baserunners to steal whenever the ball is in play, but official rules in many school leagues and amateur leagues limit or do not allow base stealing or lead-offs (stepping off the base onto the basepath before the ball is pitched). Check the rules as they apply to your own league.

There are few more exciting moments than the base steal. Even just threatening to steal can be a good strategy. It can distract the pitcher from concentrating totally on the batter. The best time to steal is when the pitcher has begun his delivery, so watch out! The pitcher might shorten his delivery style, losing his wind-up and going directly into the set position. He may try for the "pick-off play," a quick throw to a baseman who'll tag you out. That's why a cautious lead-off is the best. Keep close enough to the base that you'll be able to touch the bag if the pitcher throws the ball in your direction.

Watch the pitcher at all times. Study every part of the pitcher's style — his starting position, his stretch, his ability to turn and throw to a baseman. You must also judge when is the best time to steal a base. Remember to consider the skills of the pitcher and the catcher, the game score, the inning, how many "outs" are made and, most important, your coach's tactics and instructions. And once you do run, hustle to the next base. If the pitch is not hit, the catcher will try to fire the ball toward the baseman. If the baseman catches the ball and touches you with it before you tag the base, you have been "caught stealing," and that's an out.

Although second, third and home base are the only bases a runner can steal, it sometimes looks as if a batter is stealing first base. The Dropped Third Strike rule allows the batter to run to first base when the catcher fumbles a third-strike pitch if: (1) it is unoccupied, or (2) if first base is occupied with two out. Should the runner reach first base before the throw from the catcher, this batter who just struck out gets to stay on base!

Some daring runners steal home plate from third base. The runner must time his break for when both the pitcher and catcher are caught off-guard or, more likely, a throw to get another baserunner out takes the attention away from him. The legendary Ty Cobb holds the all-time record of stealing home 35 times. And then there's Lou Brock of the St. Louis Cardinals, who stole 938 bases — without ever once stealing home plate!

THE CATCHER

Known as "a team's spark plug," the catcher has a great view of the action. It's all directly in front of him! This is why the catcher is in a good position to be the on-field manager. You can direct the fielders to move according to where the batter might place the ball. Call out the game situation as it develops and help focus the players on key strategies for each play, such as "One out, double play at second," "Throw is to third" or "Count is two and one. Watch for the steal." The more information that you pass along to your team players, the better prepared they are to react.

Practice catching balls thrown low that hit the dirt in front of you. You'll prevent a lot of extra base runs — and build your pitcher's trust.

If there is a disputed call on a play, don't argue with the umpire. It's better to stay on good terms with someone you're working so closely with!

You can also watch the baserunners communicate with their coaches and anticipate a "surprise" move.

The catcher always directs the pitcher's throw to each batter. Before each game, scouting reports are consulted. The manager and coaches discuss the abilities of each batter on the opposing team and what pitches will work best against them.

When the game starts, it's up to you to signal to the pitcher before he throws what kind of pitch and where it should be thrown — high, low, inside or outside. The fewer and simpler the signals, the better. Practice them ahead of time with the pitcher. Signal with your hand against your inner thigh. This hides the signals from the batter and the base coaches. Stolen signs can result in lots of hits by the opposing team.

Get to know each pitcher. If his throw is lacking in control, or he's not settling into a smooth manner, ask the umpire for a time-out, go to the mound and offer the pitcher some encouragement. Your words of support could boost the pitcher's confidence and delay his substitution.

The Stance

Try to be as close as you can to the plate without getting in the way of the swing. Catching the ball near to the plate gives the umpire less opportunity to judge if a pitch went wide before it was caught.

Crouch down with your legs apart. Lean forward and balance on the balls of your feet.

Hold your glove hand steady and aimed at the pitcher. Signal to the pitcher with your bare hand hidden by your legs, and then clench that hand into a fist beside your glove. Stay still when the pitcher winds up: your glove is now his target.

The Plays

From the crouch position, you're always ready to jump up and field the ball.

When catching high pop fouls behind the plate area, pull off your mask and throw it back where you won't trip on it. Think about the direction of the wind and any shadows. Raise your mitt above your head and trap the ball.

Tagging a runner at home plate takes concentration. Keep a foot on the plate as you wait for the throw from a fielder. When you have caught the ball, put your bare hand over the pocket to stop the ball from being kicked loose, lean forward toward third base and touch that part of the runner's body that is closest to reaching home plate.

A snap throw to second base can stop a runner on the steal. Use the momentum as you rise from your crouch stance to launch the throw. Don't extend your arm out for the throw — it should be in tight passing your head.

If there's a short bunt and third base is unoccupied, jump onto the field, snag the ball in your glove, pull it out and fire it on to the first baseman.

If third base is unoccupied, you must also "back up" throws from the outfield to first base. Move to an area behind the base. That way you're in a position to stop any ball that is dropped or thrown wide.

THE PITCHER

"An ace in the diamond's center," the pitcher most often holds the fate of the game. Great pitching wins; bad pitching loses.

Keeping in good physical condition and practicing ball control will keep you alert and confident in every game situation. For a review on the mechanics of pitching, see the previous chapter. Successful pitching demands total concentration. During the game, maintain communication with the catcher. Focus your attention on the catcher's signals and target glove.

Forget about the batter: he can't do a thing until you throw the ball. But if there are runners on base, look at them — more than once so they know you haven't forgotten about them. It will shorten their lead-off.

Practice throwing to a low area in the strike zone, as these pitches give batters the biggest problem. They can't see a low pitch as easily as if it was coming in closer to their eye level. Throwing lots of low strikes is the sign of a great pitcher.

Try to expand your duties during practice so you can recover short hits and bunts, and know your role during each defensive play. A pitcher who becomes the "fifth infielder" gives his team a huge advantage.

Knowing your team's exact defensive status before each pitch also keeps you clear on the strategy of every throw and prepares you to react if the ball is hit. How many "out"? Are there runners on base? Which bases? Who is most likely to steal? Where does the ball get thrown on a bunt? Or on a pop-fly?

Try to make your first pitch a strike. Don't center it over the plate, but put it in such a spot that the batter can't resist swinging at it. With that first strike, you are "ahead of the batter" and the pressure shifts onto him. Only two of your next five pitches need to be in the strike zone for an "out." If you "get behind on the batter," you may tense up and make mistakes. A count of 2–0 (two balls, no strikes) or 3–1 (three balls, one strike) gives the batter a choice of what he hits. He can wait to swing at the kind of pitch he most likes to hit.

The Pitching Squad

It is not very common these days for a pitcher to work a "complete game," throwing for nine innings. The manager usually has a strategy for using different pitchers at different times.

The "starter" begins the game and usually throws for five or six innings. He needs four or five days of rest between assignments, so a typical squad includes about five starters.

The relief pitcher or reliever comes in when the starter begins to lose his edge. The reliever works in the middle of the game. He pitches for a few innings, or may even see the game through to the end.

The "stopper" or "fireman" is a special reliever who will pitch in a tense situation when the other team is "too hot." He's expected to "put out their fire," hold

their men on bases and get his team safely out of the inning before further damage occurs. He may be used to pitch to one player or for one inning, or stay on to pitch more than that inning.

The "closer" or "terminator" goes to the mound in the second-last or final inning to protect his team's lead. This pitcher usually throws the hardest balls, but because of the strain this causes on his arm, he does not pitch any more than two innings.

Left Versus Right

The hand a pitcher throws with can make a big difference in his success against a hitter. Batters have trouble hitting balls that are moving away from them. When a left-handed pitcher throws a curve ball to a left-handed batter, the ball swerves away from the batter; this gives the pitcher an advantage. A right-handed pitcher has the same advantage throwing against a right-handed hitter. A manager may use this as a strategy during a game. It happens when he puts in a relief pitcher who throws from the same side that the batter hits from.

The Plays

Let another infielder make the catch on most pop-fly balls, but you should chase any short bunts or weak pop-ups that drop in front of the mound.

If a bunt or grounder is hit to the left of the mound, run immediately to first base. This allows the first baseman to move from the base, stop the ball, turn and throw it to you as — ideally! — you step on the base ahead of the runner.

Covering other bases as a backup, in case of a fumble or over-throw, completes your role as a "fifth infielder." In general, you should cover behind third base, first base or home plate for throws from the outfield. But your primary responsibility is behind home plate, to cover on the big throws or during rundowns.

The Pitch-out Play

Timed well, the pitch-out is a great defensive move. If a catcher steals a signal from a base coach or senses that a runner is about to steal a base, he signals for a pitch-out. You will throw wide to the unoccupied batter's box. The batter is prevented by the rules from stepping out of his own box to try hitting the lob. The catcher is standing and ready to fire the ball back toward the base where the runner is heading.

When the manager calls for the batter to be given an intentional walk, you will throw the ball to the same area.

The Pick-off Play

An alert pitcher can hold a runner on base longer and limit him to the shortest possible lead-off by threatening a pick-off play. If you see the runner taking a few too many lead-off steps from the base or moving back to the base when you glance at him, go into action. Forget the wind-up and go directly into the set position. Keep your movement to a minimum to avoid a balk (see below). Turn quickly and deliver a sharp, knee-high throw to the baseman's glove. Fast timing, and lots of practice with the baseman, will get the out.

The Balk

A balk can occur only when there are one or more base-runners and is illegal. The pitcher balks when he does not step toward a base during a pick-off play; pitches without one foot on the mound's rubber; stands on the rubber and either touches his bare hand to his mouth or drops the ball onto the mound; pretends to pitch without having the ball; or suddenly stops the delivery.

All runners are allowed to advance one base.

After the Game

Clean off and cool down with a shower. Use the warm water to soothe your pitching shoulder and arm. If swelling begins, put your arm in a sink or bucket of cold water, then wrap on an ice pack and take it easy. Rest your arm for a day or two before you start throwing some easy pitches. Remember: never throw the ball — even in practice — if your arm is sore.

Once they have control of the ball, Major League pitchers are allowed just 20 seconds to throw the next pitch. If there is too much of a delay, the umpire can give a warning and call a ball if the delay continues. However, if there are baserunners, there is no time limit as long as the pitcher keeps the game moving and does not deliberately delay the game. He may attempt pick-off plays between pitches.

Between 1899 and 1911, the great Cy Young completed 749 games of the 815 he started!

Walter "Big Train" Johnson completed 531 games out of the 660 times he took to the mound as a starter.

Joe "Iron Man" McGinnity pitched 434 innings for the New York Giants during one season. This still stands as a National League record. In that same year, 1903, the Iron Man also pitched both games of a doubleheader — 18 continuous innings — three separate times in one month!

In 1915, Walter "Big Train" Johnson was said to throw so hard that batters never saw the ball — they could only hear it roaring past them like a locomotive!

A 17-year-old Bob Feller came to the Majors in 1936 based on astonishing reports from a pitching scout. Feller practiced by throwing the ball with such force against the side of the family barn that he kept knocking holes through the boards!

The most recent "fastest pitch" challenge comes with scientific proof: a police radar gun, normally used on speeding vehicles. In the 1985 All-Star Game, both Nolan Ryan and Goose Gossage had fastballs clocked at 103 mph!

THE FIRST BASEMAN

Most "outs" in a game happen at first base. With all that action, a sturdy and reliable player with a long reach is the ideal first baseman. Because he must be able to catch every kind of ball — high, low, wide or in the dirt — that can possibly be thrown by an infielder and still keep a foot secured to the base, the first baseman is known as the "anchor of the infield."

The Stance

All infielders prepare for a hit with the same stance. Bend your knees, lean forward and balance on the balls of your feet. Hold your glove low and opened toward home plate.

With no runner at first, stand about eight feet away from the bag along the baseline or back farther at the edge of the outfield, depending upon the defensive situation. This will give you plenty of room to stop balls coming through the right side of the infield.

The Plays

During regular play, return to your base as soon as the ball is hit to another fielder. Plant the toe of your left foot on the edge of the base closest to the mound and s-t-r-e-t-c-h for the ball. Catch it as far out in front of the base as you can. Not only will you reach the ball sooner, but you will keep out of the way of a baserunner who is running wide.

The Pick-off Move

With a runner on first who is taking a lead-off, you must guard the base. Point both feet toward the pitcher. Position your left foot on the baseline from home and your right foot on the edge of the bag.

On the catch, turn toward the right so that you can tag the runner if he returns to the base. Make contact with the part of his body that is closest to the base. Even if he gets back safely, tag him. It's good practice for you, and it will show him you have steady reflexes!

As the pitcher commits to a throw home, quickly shift from this pick-off position to your regular fielding position. You'll be ready to run in to pick up a bunt or roller, or to step back on base for an infielder's throw.

If the pitch is not hit, return to the pick-off position to guard the base.

Other Plays

The first baseman is responsible for all balls hit or bunted to your infield side of the pitcher's mound. When you leave your base and go after them, the pitcher covers first base. When you catch the ball, an underhand toss toward the pitcher's chest may get the runner out on first.

On throws from deep center or right field, you become the cut-off man. Place yourself near the mound. If the throw seems to be off the mark, run to catch it before it goes astray, then relay it quickly to the correct base.

Be alert for foul balls to your side of the field. An alert first baseman takes them for an easy "out."

A pop-fly can be an automatic out — even if a fielder drops it. In 1895, the Official Baseball Rules added the Infield Fly rule. It saves baserunners from being the victims of unsporting play. The rule prevents a fielder from "accidentally" fumbling a flyball so that a force-out or double play can be set up and get more players out than just the single out that catching the fly would count for.

The Infield Fly rule is called when the bases are loaded or there are runners on first and second, and the inning has fewer than two outs. If the batter hits a pop-fly ball that is not a result of a bunt into fair territory and the umpire believes it can be easily caught, he calls out "Infield fly if ball is fair!" After the call, the runners hold their positions on base and the batter is out.

THE SECOND BASEMAN

Second base is known as the "keystone" or "marker," because runners at second have a good chance of reaching home on an outfield hit. Second base is also the pivot point for most double plays.

The second baseman acts as a rover. His position on the field varies for each hitter and according to the defensive situation. The second baseman and the shortstop are the "keystone combination." They work as partners to control the middle infield play. Lots of practice and good teamwork let each player know in advance exactly what the other one is going to do.

The Stance

The second baseman uses the infield stance. Crouch slightly with your knees bent, balance on the balls of your feet, and hold your glove near the ground and open toward the batter.

Practice quick sidestep movements with one foot scissoring in front of the other. This lets you move toward a ball hit to one side without turning from the play. And if the ball has a bad bounce, your body will be in a better position to block it.

The Plays

Talk to the shortstop about who covers the field and who covers second base as each batter comes to the plate. This constant communication makes for smooth plays and a minimum of mistakes.

A second baseman is like an extra shortstop. When a ball is hit to the left-field side, your job is to cover second base. In most cases, you'll be responsible for catching pop-flys and ground balls hit between second and first base. This allows the first baseman to wait at his base for the throw. The shortstop will move over to cover second base.

When a hit goes into right field, move toward it. If the outfielder gets into difficulty, you're ready to help. When the ball is recovered, place yourself at the edge of the outfield so that you can cut off or relay the throw.

On a bunt down the right side, race over to cover first. The first baseman will already be after the ball. He'll throw it to you to get the runner out on first.

The Basic Double Play

A double play gets two "outs" on a single hit and can take the heat off a tense inning.

When there's a runner on first and the batter makes a hit, there are two possible plays for you to make. If it's hit between second and first base you will likely field the ball. You'll move to stop the ball and throw it to the shortstop at second base. If there is a hit to the left field, you'll likely make a pivot play. You'll go to second to catch the ball from another fielder for the first out. Then you'll hurl it over to first base to get the hitter out. Lots of practice tunes up your ability to catch the ball, touch the base, step out of the way of the runner, then complete the play by throwing to first base — all in one fluid motion.

The Rundown Play

Sometimes a baserunner makes a wrong move. Maybe he tried to run too far on a hit, then found himself facing the ball at the next stop. Maybe he started to steal and halted on the basepath, wondering whether to run forward or back.

A runner stuck in this "hot box" can be tagged out in a rundown. For example, if a player is caught between first and second base, you'll go after the runner for a tag. The shortstop will cover second base, and the pitcher will hurry over to cover the first baseman from behind as the backup.

You are now the rundown man. Force the runner back to first base. When the runner starts for first, toss the ball to the first baseman. The runner will likely stop, then dart back toward second. The first baseman chases him for a short distance. If the runner swirls around again, the first baseman will tag him while the pitcher covers first base.

If the runner continues toward second, the first baseman tosses the ball to the shortstop, who is now standing in front of second base. The shortstop advances toward the runner with the ball. The centerfielder moves in behind you to cover second base. The shortstop may fake a throw to the baseman behind the runner. If the runner hesitates, the shortstop stretches forward to tag the runner "out."

For the play to work best, the fielders should stay inside the baseline for this catch-and-throw. It will keep you in line, which helps to prevent hitting the runner with the ball.

The rundown strategy is to force the runner back to his original base so that even if the tag fails and the runner is not out, he hasn't gained another base.

THE SHORTSTOP

A shortstop covers the widest range of duties on a baseball team. He is usually responsible for the fielding territory between second and third base, but he has to keep alert and moving. On many plays he shares coverage of second base, he can relay the ball to third base on right field hits and he backs up third on throws and some bunts. He is also the catcher's assistant: by watching the signs passed from the catcher to the pitcher, the short-stop can alert the other fielders as to what kind of ball is being thrown, which makes it easier to predict where it may be hit. Sometimes he can even read the opponents' signs and prepare his teammates for a bunt, a steal or a hit-and-run.

No wonder the shortstop is known as the player who is always on the move!

The Stance

The shortstop's stance is the infielder's crouch position. Be ready to go for hits to your left or right side. Hold your glove so you'll be ready to grab any sharp ground-ers that hit the infield fast and hard.

The Plays

The shortstop and the second baseman are the "key-stone combination." They work together to give a team solid defense.

When there's a hitter up and a runner on first, the double play often includes the shortstop. If the ball is hit toward right field, you go to cover second. The throw will come here to you. Touch the base, then step off and fire the ball to first for the other out.

If a grounder is hit, move to snap it up and throw it all in one move to the second baseman, who should be covering his own base. The second baseman completes the double play by throwing to first.

You are the tagger on a steal from first or a pick-off play at second. Getting on the bag quickly to beat the runner and take the catcher's long throw calls for a fast response. So does a tag on a runner leading off from second base. Practice this move with the pitcher to make it work successfully.

A hit to the outfield brings you into play as a cut-off man for third base. Position yourself between the fielder throwing the ball and its target. If the throw falls short, or needs redirecting toward another base, you are in position to catch the ball and move it quickly.

Scoot in to call the catch on foul balls hit beyond third base that are too shallow for the left fielder to reach.

The Hit-and-Run Play

With a quick baserunner at first, and an accurate batter at the plate, the manager might signal a "hit-and-run." It is a gamble for the hitting team. As the pitcher begins his delivery, the runner at first races toward second. Now it's the job of the batter to connect with whatever ball is thrown and hit safely. If he doesn't, the runner may be tagged out by the catcher's snap throw to second. When it all works properly, the runner is at third base — or home! — and the batter has gone to first.

How can your "keystone combination" break up the hit-and-run? Try to predict your opponents' strategy. Don't move out of position when you see the stealing runner. If either you or the second baseman race back to cover second base, you'll leave a big gap open for the batter to hit through. Wait until the batter connects. Then the one closest to the ball fields it, while the other goes to cover second.

The safest way to tag a runner is to use your bare hand to hold the ball in the glove after catching it. Then go to the front of the base and allow the runner to come in to the glove. Once contact has been made, pull your hands away immediately. If you reach toward the runner with the ball in your glove, the ball might be knocked loose and the runner would be safe.

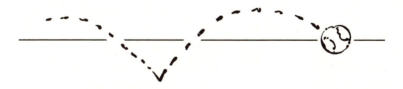

THE THIRD BASEMAN

The third baseman is on "the hot corner" because so many bullet-like hits rip here from just 90 feet away. The third baseman must be able to stop fast grounders or line drives and then launch a long, accurate throw across to first base.

Because most batters are right-handed, more hits travel to the left side of the field. The third baseman not only helps the shortstop close the big gap over to second base but must be ready for hits straight down the baseline.

Ignore your pitcher during his wind-up and delivery. All your concentration must be fixed on the batter. Quick reaction to a hit means the difference between an "out" and a runner getting on base.

The Stance

Prepare for the hit by going into the infielder's crouch. Since speedy reactions are needed on this busy corner, hold your glove out low and in front of the body for fielding grounders and keep an eye on the ball until it is in the glove.

The Plays

Never step back to grab a ground ball. If there's a runner storming to first base, you don't have time. Always advance toward the ball.

When there is a runner going for home plate during a close game, throw to home. If there is a good chance of making a double play, throw to second.

On a force play to third, just step on the bag. Since two runners cannot occupy one base, the lead runner is forced to advance to the next base on each safe hit or bunt. When there are runners at first and second base, you can expect to field a nearby hit yourself. Make the catch and simply step on the bag to "force out" the runner coming from second.

In general, your throws will be going to first base. Practicing long, accurate throws to first base keeps the "hot corner man" in shape to keep his team hotter.

A third baseman must be in the right place at the right time. It helps if you think about the other team's tactics and know each hitter's abilities, and if you keep aware of the game situation, such as the number of "outs," the score and what inning it is. Is a bunt likely? If there are baserunners, play close to your baseline and well inside the infield so that you can charge the ball. If the other bases are occupied, stay near third base for the force-out. The pitcher will cover your zone along the baseline. If there is a right-handed pull hitter at the plate with no one on base, stand beyond the basepath just out of the infield.

The third baseman is also the "lookout man" of his team. Watch carefully to make certain that every base is touched by a runner, especially at third. Many times, it is the third baseman's call for an appeal play on a runner who has failed to touch the bases or to tag up that results in an "out" (see p. 90).

Both the cut-off play and the relay play can prevent a run being scored and stop a runner from getting extra bases on an outfield hit.

For the cut-off play, an infielder positions himself between the outfield thrower and the target. From here, he is available to intercept the throw and redirect the ball to another base when needed.

On the relay play, an infielder moves into the same position between the outfield thrower and the target, but he knows in advance that the throw will be coming to him. His job is to catch the throw, spin around and send it on to the target base. The relay man breaks up a long throw that may not reach its mark and makes the "out" a surer thing.

THE OUTFIELDERS

Outfielders don't make as many fast and daring plays as those in the infield. In fact, outfielders get more attention for their batting records than they do for any fielding skills. But while a batter might come to the plate four or five times during a game, an outfielder plays his position every inning for a whole game. Obviously, such a player has to do more than hit.

As an outfielder, you must have the ability to catch long flyballs, to stop grounders and to quickly make a big throw back into the infield. An accurate throw by an outfielder can hold a runner on base as easily as a pop-fly caught by the shortstop.

A good outfielder is also known as "an assistant infielder." That's because you back up every hit made to the infield or every throw made by the catcher to the basemen. The general rule is for the rightfielder to be the first-base backup, the centerfielder to be the second-base backup and the leftfielder to be the third-base backup.

It helps to examine the conditions of the ballpark before the game gets under way. That way you'll play without any need to hesitate about the surroundings. What direction is the wind blowing? Are there any shifting patterns caused by walls or the park design? How far is the warning track from the wall or back fence? How far can the back fence be climbed to get some added height for grabbing a flyball?

The Plays

You must always be ready to change your position in the outfield according to which hitter is at bat. For example, when there is a pull hitter at the plate, the outfielders will shift positions to be more in line with the direction in which the batter usually hits. Your coach will direct you to play farther back or closer to the infield.

When to throw at a relay man requires quick thinking. If a baserunner is going for an extra bag on a bouncer to the outfield and you are throwing from deep near the fence, you might decide to aim the ball at the relay man. Let him catch it chest-high, so that he can quickly spin around and relay the throw.

Call It!

The golden rule of all fielders — especially those in the outfield — is to "call the ball" when it's hit. When the ball reaches the top of its arc and starts coming down toward the ground, the fielder who has the best chance of catching it should yell out "It's mine!" or "I've got it!"

Always let the fielder who made the call make the play. You'll avoid a collision and you'll be in a position to recover the ball quickly and get it back into play if the ball is fumbled or missed.

"Strength down the middle" refers to those players on a direct line with home plate: catcher, pitcher, shortstop, second baseman and centerfielder. These are the main elements of a defensive team.

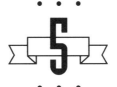

Keeping the Game Going

As long as you have enough players and the right equipment, you can play a game of baseball. But it doesn't hurt to have umpires on hand to make the calls. And every Major League team has a manager, coaches and scouts to build their squad and keep it hot.

THE UMPIRE

"It's nothing until I call it!" — Bill Klem, umpire

Umpires have the hardest job in baseball: they must make correct calls all the time. That's why an umpire needs great eyesight and shrewd judgment. Only rarely is the umpire's original decision changed after a "debate" on the field. That's because the umpire is almost always correct when judging a close play.

Umpires endure a lot of verbal abuse from players, coaches and fans. They must avoid getting involved in arguments. If anyone on the field pushes or attempts to hurt the umpire, that person can be disqualified from the game at once. Depending upon the seriousness of the offence, further penalties and a suspension can be imposed.

Before the Game

The umpire has a dirty job, especially preparing for the game. He rubs sixty brand-new, clean baseballs with a special mud. This takes the smooth shine off the ball. The pitcher can get a better grip on the ball and the batter can see it more easily.

Then the umpires check the playing field. Are all the bases secure? Is the dirt around each base level and even? Are the chalk lines for the batter's box and the basepaths clear? Is the field free of any holes or dips that could cause an injury?

The starting line-up, which lists the batting order and the player positions, is given to the umpire at home plate by the coaches. Substitutions to the line-up cannot occur unless the umpire is notified.

Working a Game

Four umpires work every regular season Major League game, one behind home plate and one at each base. The umpire behind home plate decides whether the pitches are balls or strikes and keeps count of them. A strike is shouted out along with a hand motion. Silence usually indicates the pitch was a ball. The plate umpire also observes if the pitcher has balked, if a runner is safe or out coming into home and whether infield hits are fair or foul. Each plate umpire may have a different interpretation of the strike zone, but he must call pitches the same way for both teams.

Base umpires primarily decide whether a runner reaches a base before the ball is caught there. They also rule on fair/foul hits down the lines, interference and tag-outs. A base umpire can be asked to make a "strike call" concerning check, or half-swings; if so, whatever he says is the final decision.

On rare occasions, two umpires might disagree over a call. The crew chief among the group then makes the final decision.

The Umpire's Signs

an out or strike

the runner is safe

foul ball or time-out

foul tip

fair play or fair ball

spectator interference

The Strike Zone

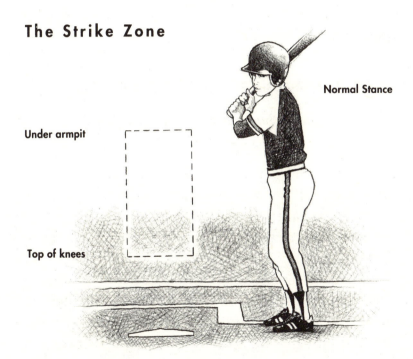

Normal Stance

Under armpit

Top of knees

Appeal Plays

Some infractions are called by the defensive team on the field. The umpire will rule on these appeal plays only when asked by a player:

- to call a penalty if the wrong batter comes to the plate;
- to call a runner "out" for failing to touch a base before advancing to another base, or for failing to touch home plate;
- to call a baserunner "out" for advancing before a flyball is caught.

The request for a decision must be made before play continues.

THE MANAGER AND COACHES

"To manage a baseball team is to orchestrate music out of nine soloists." — Joey Grandford, sports fan

Every baseball team is a collection of expert athletes. To coordinate all of these specialists, each Major League team has a variety of coaches and assistants who are under the direction of the head coach, the team manager.

The manager is responsible for the overall strategy of the team. He chooses the starting line-up and decides when to call in substitutions. The manager relies upon all of his coaches for advice in meetings, practices and during games. By collecting specific information from the coaches, the manager builds a team that uses the best talents of each player.

Batting coaches work with the hitters. They help players refine their swing, stride and even their bunting technique. Players in a batting slump look to these experts for guidance and objective tips.

Pitching coaches study the form and delivery of every pitcher on their squad. They help the pitchers keep fastballs consistent and curveballs accurate. They evaluate the strength and weakness of each pitcher so they will match them up against the opposing teams' batters. The bullpen coaches work with pitchers in the warm-up area before they enter a game. They pass along information to the pitchers about the hitters they will confront.

First-base and third-base coaches stand on the field during games to advise their runners. They must know their players' running ability, the strength of a fielder's throwing arm and the opponent's strategy. They tell a runner how far to lead off from the base. When a ball is hit, they calculate its speed and landing location and they shout for the runner to slide, to hold, to take one or two bases or to run for home plate. They also pass signals along from the manager to the batter ordering a hit or bunt or to "take" the pitch and not swing at all.

The system of signs and signals has been established before the game begins. In one inning, the batter may know to pay attention only to the second sign coming from the third-base coach. All other signs are meant to confuse the opposing team. The manager in the dugout may send a set of signals to the base coaches, who then signal the runner to attempt to steal the next base.

Communication between the manager and coaches remains vital through the game. The individual skills of the players are "managed" like figures on a chessboard arranged to win through a series of tactical moves.

THE SCOUTS

Major League baseball teams use three types of scouts. A "free-agent" scout looks for amateur players who show promise of becoming big-leaguers. He'll look for prospects at the high school and collegiate level. This scout may also travel to a rural area to see a game played in haphazard conditions, and then go to a city where a "hot tip" leads him to a young man throwing fastball strikes against a mail box.

Because organized amateur leagues give players a chance to work on their skills, it is easiest for a scout to assess baseball potential during scheduled games.

The minor professional league is the home of the farm team system. The teams in these operations survive through local community support and with money from Major League teams who own the players' contracts. The "minor pro" scouts analyze the skills on display of those players hoping to fulfill a dream to soon go up to the Majors.

An "advance" scout travels ahead of his team to observe an upcoming opponent. He draws pitching charts to show who is throwing what kind of ball and how often it has been hit, and batting charts to illustrate what each batter swings at and where the ball goes. He also will study the other team's tactics by watching their fielding, baserunning and stealing techniques.

This information is then sent to the manager and his coaches, who use it to decide on their own strategy for playing against that particular team.

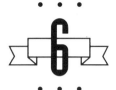

The Major Leagues: National and American

Major League baseball today refers to the National League and the American League. The National League was organized in 1876. It had eight founding members: the Philadelphia Athletics, the New York Mutuals, the Chicago White Stockings, the Cincinnati Red Stockings, the St. Louis Browns, the Boston Red Caps, the Hartford Dark Blues and the Louisville Grays.

Major changes occurred in the 1950s, when some teams expanded westward. The Brooklyn Dodgers transformed into the Los Angeles Dodgers in 1958, the same year that New York's other National League team, the Giants, was reborn as the San Francisco Giants.

In 1969, the Montreal Expos became the first Major League club located outside of the United States.

Due to continued expansion, plus the desire to create more regional rivalries, both leagues have split into three divisions.

The current National League teams are:

NL East Division	NL Central Division	NL West Division
Atlanta Braves	Chicago Cubs	Colorado Rockies
Florida Marlins	Cincinnati Reds	Los Angeles Dodgers
Montreal Expos	Houston Astros	San Diego Padres
New York Mets	Pittsburgh Pirates	San Francisco Giants
Philadelphia Phillies	St. Louis Cardinals	

When the National League refused to admit other teams to its organization around the turn of the century, those frustrated players and owners formed the American League in 1901. Charlie Comiskey moved a team from St. Paul, Minnesota, to become the Chicago White Sox. Other founding clubs were the Milwaukee Brewers, the Boston Somersets, the Cleveland Blues, the Detroit Tigers, the Washington Senators, the Baltimore Orioles and the Philadelphia Athletics.

The current American League teams are:

AL East Division	AL Central Division	AL West Division
Baltimore Orioles	Chicago White Sox	California Angels
Boston Red Sox	Cleveland Indians	Oakland Athletics
Detroit Tigers	Kansas City Royals	Seattle Mariners
New York Yankees	Milwaukee Brewers	Texas Rangers
Toronto Blue Jays	Minnesota Twins	

The National League and the American League play each other on only three occasions during the year: in exhibition matches during spring training, for the All-Star Game and in the World Series.

However there are discussions about the possibility of interleague games becoming part of the regular season (for example, N.Y. Yankees vs. N.Y. Mets; Toronto Blue Jays vs. Montreal Expos; Chicago Cubs vs. Chicago White Sox, etc.)

An agreement exists among the owners of teams in both leagues to give the final authority on all matters to the Commissioner of Baseball. They also observe rules and regulations concerning player trades between leagues or teams in each division and the rights of minor league players. Other rules in the agreement protect teams from losing a player who wants to go elsewhere unless that player has legally concluded his primary contract.

The Commissioner of Baseball discusses issues with both the National League President and the American League President. They have the final decision on scheduling games, determining the World Series timetable and presenting changes to the rules. Together they ensure that the standards of umpires, fair play and proper conduct are upheld.

When a lot of Major League players went off to fight in World War II, teams such as the Cincinnati Red Legs were left with lots of young players. In 1944, the Red Legs sent Joe Nuxhall to the mound. The 15-year-old became the youngest person ever to play in a Major League game. He pitched less than an inning and gave up five runs.

Although this was not a great start, Nuxhall returned to the Majors in 1952 and pitched for the next 14 years. He retired with a respectable ERA of 3.90, pitched 20 shutout games and as a batter got 15 home runs!

The Championship
Season

The push for the World Series starts long before the regular baseball season even begins.

In late February every year, each team sets up a training camp to look over new recruits and to get the veterans back in shape. This month-long session readies the team for the grueling daily schedule of playing ball for the next half-year. The coaching staff hires some players and cuts others or sends them back down to the minors so that the best possible talent stays in the line-up.

Skills are tested and developed. Exhibition games are held with other pro teams so that the performance of new players can be judged.

A team plays 162 games during the regular season. The team with the best win/loss average finishes at the top of its division.

In the last weeks of September, the race for the division championship heats up and the "magic number" usually makes its appearance in the newspapers. The "magic number" helps fans keep track of the progress of the first-place team. It is a calculation of two things: wins and losses. If the magic number is eight, the first-place Team X will win the division if it wins eight games, or if second-place Team Y loses eight, or any combination of wins and losses that equal eight.

But if Team Y loses three games, then the magic number becomes five; to conquer the division, the first-place Team X now only needs a combination of wins by itself and losses by Team Y that total five.

Here's another way to fathom the magic number: you want to finish the season so that you are at least two games ahead of your closest rival with only one game left to play in the season. Therefore, even if you lose and they win in that final game, you are still one game up on them in the overall standings.

THE PENNANT

Many fans believe that it is when the regular season ends that the real baseball season begins! In each league, the three division winners and a "wild card" team (the second-place team with the best overall record) will pair off for a best-of-five games playoff. The two finalists then compete in a best-of-seven games

League Championship Series to win the Pennant. This decides the top team in the American League and National League for that year, who then go on to play the best-of-seven games for the World Series.

The Mystery Behind the Magic Number:

Here's how the league standings might be in late September:

	Wins	Losses	
Toronto	90	62	(with 10 games remaining)
Baltimore	86	66	

To find Toronto's Magic Number:

(A) Add "one" to the number of games remaining in the schedule for the top team.

(B) Look at the "loss" column in the league standings: how many games is the top team ahead of its nearest competitor?

$$(A) - (B) = \text{Magic Number}$$

A is $1 + 10 = 11$

B is $66 - 62 = 4$

$$11 - 4 = 7$$

The Jays' magic number is 7.

Thus, any combination of Jays wins and Baltimore losses totaling 7 clinches the division title for Toronto.

THE WORLD SERIES

The World Series is a unique sporting championship because it is the only one that is played between two teams who have never competed against each other in the regular season.

The World Series tradition began in 1903, when the Boston Pilgrims beat the Pittsburgh Pirates. Now the media blitz of this "Fall Classic" blankets all of North America, while the rest of the world tunes in on satellite TV.

Only one adjustment needs to be made for players in the World Series. That concerns the role of the "designated hitter."

Most pitchers make poor hitters. In fact, umpires have been known to laugh at their efforts in the batter's box. In 1973, the American League decided to spare their players and fans from further humiliation. They introduced the Designated Hitter rule, which allows each team to substitute a non-fielding player to bat for the pitcher. As a result, the batting order covers up what used to be a weak link in the chain. The National League, however, continues to let its pitchers bat.

What happens when the two leagues meet in the World Series?

The ruling now states that when a Series game is played in a National League park, there will be no designated hitter. American League pitchers who haven't held a bat in years must go into the batting order and take a turn at the plate. Of course, when the game is played in an American League park, the National League team gets to substitute its pitcher in the batting order.

The World Series presents the best opportunity for players to show their full talent. And with the biggest audience of the baseball season watching, it's a perfect occasion for some magical moments.

The New York Yankees have won the most World Series. They have captured 21 World Series titles since their first win in 1923. They have also won the American League Pennant 33 times.

After its 1903 beginning, the World Series seemed to be a way for the National and American leagues to resolve their differences. But nobody told that to the owners of the National League's 1904 Pennant winners, the New York Giants. They refused to let their team play against the contending champs, the Boston Pilgrims, who they felt represented a "brash, minor league."

However, opinions soon changed. The following year, the Giants did agree to participate, and they beat Philadelphia in five games.

THE ALL-STAR GAME

The Century of Progress Exposition, or "Expo," held in Chicago in 1933 did more than highlight technical wonders to the world. It gave the National League and the American League a chance to field their best players against each other in the first All-Star Game.

Babe Ruth hit a two-run homer in the third inning, leading the American League to a 4–2 win over the National. (And the top ticket price at Comiskey Park was $1.10!)

Today, the All-Star Game is part of a three-day celebration in July that brings the past and present together. The game provides a chance for everyone involved with the sport to take a break from the regular schedule and compare notes, players and strategies. Hall of Fame stars and past heroes of the game play a three-inning match to show the young fans how their sparkling talents have lasted. A home-run derby thrills the audience with booming hits launched off easy pitches.

Fans choose the All-Star players in a vote by ballot. The pitching squad is selected by the managers and coaches from both leagues. All the money raised through gate receipts and television rights is donated to charities and the players' pension fund.

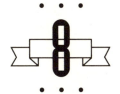

Major Events in Baseball History

- In 1845, Alexander Cartwright establishes the rules of modern baseball.
- The Cincinnati Red Stockings become the first professional baseball team. For the inaugural 1869 season, player Harry Wright is paid $1,200.
- The National League is formed in 1876.
- The American League appears in 1901.
- The first World Series brings a peaceful understanding between the National League and the American League. In this eight-game encounter in 1903, Boston beat Pittsburgh.
- Eight Chicago White Sox players are bribed to lose the 1919 World Series. The "Black Sox Scandal" awakened everyone to the fact that what was once a game had become big business.

- The Spitball is outlawed in 1920. However, pitchers who juiced the ball before that time were allowed to continue throwing the spitters; the ruling applied to all pitchers coming into the leagues after the ban.
- In the 1927 season, Babe Ruth hits 60 home runs in 151 games, a record that still stands. His Yankee teammate, Lou Gehrig, knocks 47 home runs. Together, their 107 homers were more than every other team's in their league! Their spots in the batting order were known as "Murderers' Row."
- Lou Gehrig hits four consecutive home runs in one game in 1932. His career total of 23 grand slams is a Major League record. (Babe Ruth slammed 16.)
- The first All-Star Game lets the best individual players from both leagues play against each other in Chicago, 1933. The American defeats the National League, 4–2.
- Night games begin in 1935 when Cincinnati's Crosley Field installs lights around the park.
- The National Baseball Hall of Fame and Museum opens in Cooperstown, New York, in 1939.
- Television's first baseball game is aired in 1939 throughout the New York area, featuring the Brooklyn Dodgers and the Cincinnati Reds.
- 1941 was the last great hitters' year. Joe DiMaggio hit for 56 consecutive games and Ted Williams batted .406, an average no one has since equaled.
- Jackie Robinson breaks the color bar and becomes the first black player in the Major Leagues. By joining the

Brooklyn Dodgers in 1947, Robinson led the way for others from the Negro League to get the widespread recognition, and money, that they deserved.

- A perfect game pitched in the World Series: Don Larsen faced 27 batters and got 27 consecutive outs, as his Yankees beat the Brooklyn Dodgers in Game 5 of the 1956 finals.

- In 1969, the New York Mets, the butt of bad jokes since they began in 1962, win the World Series. From nine and a half games behind the leading team in early August, they blossomed into a team who could do no wrong. They won 100 games, the National League Championship and took the World Series in five games.

- In 1971, Philadelphia Phillies pitcher Rick Wise hits two home runs and — in the same game — he also pitches a no-hitter.

- The First Strike of the 1972 season is called outside of the ballpark. For the first time baseball players go on strike and refuse to play unless their pension fund is upgraded.

- The American League in 1973 introduces the Designated Hitter rule.

- Free Agency allows players to negotiate with any team once their current contracts expire.

- In 1974, Hank Aaron surpasses Babe Ruth's total of 714 home runs. Over 24 seasons he averaged 33 homers and 100 RBIs a year.

- In 1982, Montreal hosts the All-Star Game, the first time it is played outside the United States.
- In 1991, 42-year-old Nolan Ryan gets his seventh career no-hitter.
- Baseball becomes an Olympic medal sport at the 1992 Summer Olympics in Barcelona, Spain.
- The World Series becomes truly international when played for the first time outside the United States. Canadians celebrate coast-to-coast when the Toronto Blue Jays win this fall classic, beating the Atlanta Braves in 6 games.

Breaking the Code

"In the seventh, he's one-for-three with a single bringing in an RBI. That puts him at .234 for the season, and a very respectable .401 with runners in scoring position. His on-base average of .319 is third on the team."

"They've brought the pitcher into the game with an ERA of 2.90 over 31 game appearances. He's given up 24 hits and 7 walks, and allowed in 11 runs, with 10 of those earned. He has struck out 20 batters in his 31 innings pitched."

"The race for the pennant gets hotter as this team leads the league with a percentage of .598. The magic number is now four."

Confused? Study the next few pages very carefully and you'll be able to decipher just what those announcers are talking about.

A baseball game, a team, a player and a season can all be reduced to a set of numbers. A glance at a series of digits can tell you what happened, and when, over the course of a game. And not just the one played last night — baseball statistics have been kept since the beginning of the century.

Every day during the baseball season, you can find these categories of statistics in the sports section of a newspaper:
• the Box Score details one particular game;
• the League Standings describe the race for first place;
• Individual Performance Statistics rank the pitchers, batters and fielders.

To break the code and understand baseball statistics, you don't have to be a math wizard. If you can count and do simple tricks on a calculator, you're all set.

THE BOX SCORE

This typical box score describes the events of a 1991 mid-season game between the Pittsburgh Pirates and the Cincinnati Reds. The Pirates won 10–6 over the Reds at Cincinnati's Riverfront Stadium.

Look at the top line: ab = at-bats, r = runs, h = hits, bi = runs batted in. Each player's position is noted after his name: c = catcher, p = pitcher, 1b = first base, 2b = second base, ss = shortstop, 3b = third base, rf = right field, cf = center field, lf = left field. Some players appear

PIRATES 10 at REDS 6

Pittsburgh	ab	r	h	bi		Cincinnati	ab	r	h	bi
Merced 1b	4	0	0	0		Doran 2b	5	1	1	2
JBell ss	5	0	0	0		Morris 1b	5	1	2	0
VnSlyk cf	3	2	0	0		Larkin ss	5	0	2	2
Bonilla 3b	4	3	4	2		Davis cf	4	1	1	0
Bonds lf	5	2	2	3		ONeill rf	5	0	0	0
Varsho rf	2	0	1	0		Hatchr lf	4	0	2	1
Redus rf	2	1	0	0		Qinones 3b	4	0	1	0
LVllere c	4	1	1	2		Sutko c	2	0	0	0
Wlkrsn 2b	3	1	1	1		Wnghm ph	1	0	1	0
Lind 2b	1	0	1	0		Power p	0	0	0	0
Walk p	3	0	1	1		Crman p	0	0	0	0
Heaton p	1	0	1	1		Layana p	0	0	0	0
McClnd ph	1	0	0	0		CMrtnz ph	1	1	1	1
Belinda p	0	0	0	0		KiGross p	2	1	0	0
Pttrson p	0	0	0	0		Myers p	0	0	0	0
						Braggs ph	1	0	0	0
						Oliver c	0	1	0	0
Totals	38	10	12	10		Totals	39	6	11	6

```
Pittsburgh      020  005  012–10
Cincinnati      003  000  012–6
```

LOB—Pittsburgh & Cincinnati 8 2b—Bonds (13), LaValliere (8), Wilkerson (5), Morris 2 (22), Hatcher (15), HR—Bonilla (9), Bonds (14), Doran (4), CMartinez (1).SB—Davis (13).SF—Wilkerson.

	IP	H	R	ER	BB	SO
Pittsburgh						
Walk W,7-1	6⅓	6	3	3	1	7
Heaton	1⅔	2	1	1	0	2
Belinda	⅔	3	2	2	1	1
Patterson S,2	⅓	0	0	0	0	1
Cincinnati						
KiGross L,2-1	5⅓	4	4	4	2	1
Myers	1⅔	4	3	3	1	0
Power	1	2	1	1	1	2
Carman	⅔	2	2	2	0	0
Layana	⅓	0	0	0	0	0

WP—Walk 2, PB—LaValliere. Umpires—Home, West; First, Winters; Second, B Gorman; Third, Gregg, T—3:08. A—42, 573 only as ph = pinch hitter. (A substitute baserunner would be listed as pr = pinch runner.)

Let's study how the fifth batter in each line-up did that day:

For Pittsburgh, Bonds is the left fielder (lf). He came to bat 5 times, scored himself at home twice, got 2 hits and batted in 3 runs.

For Cincinnati, O'Neill, who plays right field (rf), came to bat 5 times and scored no runs, hits or runs batted-in.

The team totals show Pittsburgh had 38 players at bat, who scored 10 runs on 12 hits, with those 10 runs batted in.

Next comes the line score, divided into groups of three innings each. It gives the inning-by-inning team scores, with the totals listed at the end of the line (i.e. Runs, Hits and Errors). Pittsburgh's big scoring (5 runs) happened in the top of the 6th inning. Cincinnati scored 3 runs in the bottom of the 3rd inning and were leading the game up until then.

A description of the batting highlights shows that both teams left on base (LOB) a total of 8 runners. Bonds was one of the players who hit to second base (2B), for his 13th time in the season. Morris got 2 doubles that day for his 22nd time. Among those getting a home run (HR) were Bonilla for his 9th time of the season and Bonds for his 14th. A stolen base (SB) was credited to Davis, for the 13th time of the season. A sacrifice fly (SF) was hit by Wilkerson.

The pitching statistics are listed in a separate chart. Pittsburgh's Bob Walk got credit for the win (W,7–1): his season record stands at 7 wins, 1 loss. He pitched 6⅓ innings (IP), allowed 6 hits (H) and let 3 runs score (R). Those three scoring runs were earned runs (ER) and were charged against his pitching average. Bob Walk gave up 1 walk or bases-on-balls (BB) and got 7 batters to strike out (SO).

Under the chart, the statistics show that a wild pitch (WP) was twice charged to Walk, and a passed ball (PB) evaded the catcher LaValliere.

Other details list the name and field position of the umpires; the time (T) of the game, this one taking 3 hours and 8 minutes to play; and the official attendance, at 42,573 fans.

Reading this box score is probably the closest thing to an eyewitness account of the game.

THE LEAGUE STANDINGS

Now take a look at the American League East Division standings for the mid-91 season. Teams are ranked from highest to lowest, based upon their percentage of wins and losses. The columns show W = games won, L = games lost, Pct = win/loss percentage, Gb = games behind the leading team, Last 10 = win/loss record for previous 10 games, Streak = how many consecutive wins/losses at

Major League Standings

American League

East

	W	L	Pct	Gb	Last 10	Streak	Home	Away
Toronto	53	35	.602	—	8–2	W1	30–17	23–18
Detroit	44	42	.512	8	6–4	W1	26–17	18–25
Boston	43	42	.506	8½	4–6	L1	24–19	19–23
New York	41	42	.494	9½	6–4	L2	22–18	19–24
Milwaukee	38	47	.447	13½	4–6	L2	22–24	16–23
Baltimore	36	49	.424	15½	5–5	W1	13–25	23–24
Cleveland	27	57	.321	24	3–7	L2	14–25	13–32

West

	W	L	Pct	Gb	Last 10	Streak	Home	Away
Minnesota	51	37	.580	—	6–4	W1	28–18	23–19
Texas	45	37	.549	3	5–5	L1	24–14	21–23
Chicago	46	39	.541	3½	6–4	W2	23–18	23–21
Oakland	47	40	.540	3½	6–4	W2	28–16	19–24
California	45	41	.523	5	2–8	L1	22–23	23–18
Seattle	44	43	.506	6½	5–5	W2	25–20	19–23
Kansas City	38	47	.447	11½	4–6	L1	15–28	23–19

present, Home = win/loss record playing at home, Away = win/loss record while playing on the road.

Here's how the New York Yankees are placed in the standings. They have won 41 games and lost 42. Add those numbers to figure out the total number of games they have played (41 + 42 = 83). Get your calculator ready to find out the Yankees' win/loss percentage. Divide the number of games played into the number of games won: dividing 83 into 41 equals .493976. Round that number to just three figures and check your answer with the chart (.494).

Notice how the Yankees are listed as 9½ games behind the league-leading Toronto Blue Jays?

Here's how that number was figured out. What is the difference between each team's wins and losses? Toronto's 53 wins is 12 more than New York's 41; the Blue Jays' 35 losses are 7 less than the Yankees' 42. Add the differences and divide that number by two:

$$12 + 7 = 19$$

$$19 \div 2 = 9\tfrac{1}{2}$$

So, for the Yankees to catch up to the Blue Jays, they have to have a lot of AB, R, H, RBIs, SB and SF!

To move up in the standings, the Yankees must win one game every time the Blue Jays lose.

The league standings can change very quickly when a team gets rolling on a streak of consecutive wins or losses. Looking at how an opponent's last 10 games have gone, as well as the record at home and away, gives other teams a quick idea of the hot/cold streak that they are coming up against.

INDIVIDUAL PERFORMANCE STATISTICS

Batting

The golden number for hitters is their batting average (AVG), or their percentage (PCT). This number represents how many hits the batter has made in his times at bat.

ST. LOUIS CARDINALS

BATTERS	AVG	OBA	AB	R	H	HR	RBI	BB	SO	SB	CS	E
Thompson	.333	.394	162	32	54	2	21	17	21	9	4	2
Jose	.311	.375	305	40	95	2	42	30	57	11	8	1
O. Smith	.307	.405	283	52	87	0	30	46	21	20	7	3
Zeile	.286	.350	304	42	87	4	38	28	49	10	6	12
Guerrero	.284	.342	289	38	82	7	53	28	25	2	1	11
Hudler	.270	.298	115	13	31	0	10	5	15	4	7	2
Pagnozzi	.261	.301	268	23	70	2	36	14	36	6	3	1
Perry	.247	.295	85	13	21	3	18	7	17	5	0	0
Lankford	.239	.282	272	39	65	1	29	16	45	21	6	4
Gilkey	.229	.336	192	16	44	3	12	31	22	10	5	0
Oquendo	.224	.357	210	15	47	1	10	44	26	1	2	5
Pena	.223	.302	94	19	21	2	7	9	24	9	4	2
Alicea	.200	.273	20	3	4	0	0	2	4	0	0	0
Wilson	.191	.235	47	4	9	0	9	3	4	0	0	1
Gedman	.116	.167	43	2	5	2	5	3	5	0	1	4
Team Totals	.261	.328	2867	360	747	29	333	291	420	108	54	52

* (Team totals provide the complete statistics of all team members for that season, including players not listed, who may have been traded or sent down to the minor league.)

Look at the St. Louis Cardinals team statistics for mid-91. The hitters are ranked according to their batting averages. Note that Ozzie Smith is third on the team. In 283 "official" at-bats (AB), Smith has had 87 hits (H). Use your calculator to divide 283 into 87 and you get .307, which is Smith's batting average.

Smith's OBA (on base average) of .405, however, leads the team. This number includes those times he got on base through walks, fielders' errors or choices, or after being struck by a pitch. A high OBA often indicates aggressive action inside the batter's box.

Other codes in the batting statistics are: SB = stolen bases, CS = caught stealing and E = errors committed while fielding.

A batting average indicates the difficulty of playing Major League baseball. Hitting at .300 means that every 100 times a player comes to bat, he gets 30 hits. That means he is successful only three times out of 10.

An excellent batting average is to hit close to .400. Boston's Ted Williams was the last player to get more than that over one season, hitting .406 back in 1941. In other words, Ted Williams missed hitting the ball successfully about six out of every ten times at bat! Can you think of any other sport where a failure rate of 60 percent is considered great?

Some at-bats don't count. If a batter comes to the plate and is walked, sacrifices or gets struck by a pitch, there has been no "official" at-bat. Therefore, the player's visit to the plate is not counted into his percentage.

Slugging Percentage

Is a triple or a double worth more than a single-base hit? The answer is no if a player's batting average is being figured out. A safe bunt onto first base counts the same as a grand slam.

But the answer is yes for a player's slugging percentage. Each base gets a point value: singles = 1, doubles = 2, triples = 3 and a home run = 4.

Let's say a player bats 14 times during a weekend series. Altogether, he hits two singles (1 + 1), a double (2) and a homer (4) for a total (1 + 1 + 2 + 4) of 8 bases.

Divide the number of times at-bat (14) into the number of bases (8) to find the players's slugging percentage (.571).

His batting average, however, registers only 4 separate hits in 14 at-bats, giving him .286 for the series.

Here's how the top three all-time slugging champs rank in comparison to their career batting averages.

THE ALL-TIME SLUGGING CHAMPS:

	Slugging Pct.	Career Batting Avg.
1. Babe Ruth	.690	.342 (#12)
2. Ted Williams	.634	.344 (#7)
3. Lou Gehrig	.632	.340 (#17)

To "hit for the cycle" is a rare achievement. A player must hit a single, a double, a triple and a home run all in one game!

Pitching

The earned run average (ERA) shows how many runs a pitcher has given up for a full nine innings pitched. The lower the ERA, the better! The number is averaged from how many total innings have been pitched and how many earned runs were given up. Earned runs are those scores that happen as a result of hits, bases-on-balls (walks) or batters hit by pitches; in other words,

through the pitcher's own doing. Runs made on fielding
errors do not count against the ERA.

PITCHERS	W	L	ERA	G	GS	SV	IP	H	R	ER	BB	SO
					BOSTON RED SOX							
Gray	2	3	2.33	43	0	1	54.0	33	15	14	9	35
Clemens	11	6	2.38	18	18	0	140.0	116	47	37	31	129
Morton	1	1	2.45	2	2	0	14.2	14	4	4	4	11
Fossas	0	1	2.59	29	0	0	24.1	14	8	7	13	12
Reardon	0	2	2.90	31	0	22	31.0	24	11	10	7	20
Lamp	3	1	3.57	22	0	0	40.1	35	19	16	13	23
Hesketh	3	1	3.74	24	2	0	55.1	51	25	23	30	43
Young	3	3	4.20	10	10	0	55.2	48	28	26	37	43
Bolton	7	6	4.62	17	15	0	85.2	108	51	44	41	48
Harris	5	8	4.64	22	15	1	97.0	95	50	50	37	71
Gardiner	3	2	4.95	6	6	0	36.1	40	22	20	13	29
Darwin	3	6	5.16	12	12	0	68.0	71	39	39	15	42
Klecker	2	1	7.20	10	4	0	25.0	36	21	20	15	13
Team Totals	43	41	3.86	84	84	24	739.0	705	349	317	272	524

Take a look at a Boston Red Sox 1991 mid-season
pitching chart. The top of the list shows those with the
best earned run average, even though there might be a
wide difference in the win/loss totals.

The abbreviations are W (win), L (loss), ERA (earned
run average), G (games), GS (games started), SV (saves),
IP (innings pitched), H (hits allowed), R (runs scored
against), ER (earned runs), BB (bases-on-balls, or walks)
and SO (strikeouts).

Let's check the ERA on Roger Clemens. Use his total
number of earned runs (37) and multiply that by 9 (for
innings per game). That comes to 333. Now take his
total number of innings pitched (140) and divide it into
333. That's how 2.38 gets to be his ERA. For every nine

innings he has pitched so far in that season, Roger Clemens has given up an average of 2.38 runs.

A pitcher who starts on the mound in the first inning will throw for all nine innings and "complete" the game or, more likely, throw for part of the game until a relief pitcher replaces him. To register a win (W), a pitcher must throw for more than five innings and leave the game only when his team is ahead in the score. And the team must win that game without losing the lead. A loss (L) goes to the pitcher who gives up the go-ahead run that results in his team's defeat.

Only a relief pitcher can get a save (SV). There are three ways that can happen:

1) He has to pitch at least one inning, and his team leads by no more than three runs.

2) He comes into the game with the potential tie run at bat, on deck or on a base.

3) The Official Scorer decides that he has pitched very well for three innings.

Today, an ERA of less than 3.00 is considered very good. The modern-day record goes to Bob Gibson of the St. Louis Cardinals for a brilliant pitching year in 1968, when he registered a 1.12 ERA.

Fielding

Statistics follow every baseball player for each part of the game. Hitters and pitchers may get the most attention, but defensive play also has its own charting.

Name	Team	B	T	GS	INN	PO	A	E	DP	PCT
Anderson	S.F.	R	R	1	19	1	2	1	0	0.750
Backman	Phi.	B	R	16	114⅔	4	25	2	1	0.935
Blauser	Atl.	R	R	12	111½	12	25	2	1	0.949
Bonilla	Pit.	B	R	49	427⅔	37	110	10	10	0.936
Caminiti	Hou.	B	R	92	809	78	175	17	18	0.937
Candaele	Hou.	B	R	3	28⅔	3	8	0	1	1.000
Coolbaugh	S.D.	R	R	51	457½	32	108	7	8	0.952
Foley	Mon.	L	R	1	23	1	5	1	0	0.857
Hamilton	L.A.	R	R	22	200	19	43	5	2	0.925
Hansen	L.A.	L	R	1	16	1	4	0	0	1.000
Harris	L.A.	L	R	63	539½	48	109	9	10	0.946
C. Hayes	Phi.	R	R	64	611	46	143	9	14	0.955
Hollins	Phi.	B	R	16	141	12	32	5	1	0.898
Jefferies	NY-N	B	R	18	160	7	33	4	1	0.909
Johnson	NY-N	B	R	73	641⅓	37	120	13	8	0.924
King	Pit.	R	R	32	281	15	62	2	0	0.975
Lemke	Atl.	B	R	2	39⅔	3	9	2	1	0.857
Litton	S.F.	R	R	5	41⅓	3	10	1	1	0.929
Pendleton	Atl.	B	R	84	723⅓	69	190	13	19	0.952
Quinones	Cin.	B	R	8	83½	4	13	1	2	0.944
Sabo	Cin.	R	R	89	777⅓	49	149	6	15	0.971

The key figure on the chart is the fielding percentage (PCT). The activities that are calculated into that are games started at the position (GS), innings played (INN), putouts or making an opposing player "out" (PO), assists (A), errors committed (E) and the double plays involved in (DP).

Like the batting average, the fielding percentage is based on a possible best of 1.000. Look at the third basemen fielding chart to calculate Pittsburgh Pirates' Bobby Bonilla's 1991 mid-season stats at third base. Add the "clean" plays — putouts and assists (37 + 110 = 147). Add the total errors to that number (10 + 147 = 157), and divide it back into the number of "clean" plays (147 ÷ 157 = .936) to get the fielding percentage. The result shows the player's statistical level of excellence on the field.

HOW TO KEEP SCORE

All of the baseball statistics published in the newspapers come from a single source: the scorecard. Every Major League game is observed by an Official Scorer who has been recommended by the home team and approved by the League Office. The scorer's duty is to record exactly what happens for each at-bat and fielding play. The Official Scorer's wide experience observing games puts him in the best position to decide whether an error has been committed during a play.

To allow the scorer to record each play, the fielding positions are numbered as 1 = pitcher, 2 = catcher, 3 = first baseman, 4 = second baseman, 5 = third baseman, 6 = shortstop, 7 = leftfielder, 8 = centerfielder and 9 = rightfielder.

The next time you hear a radio announcer report "That was a classic 6, 4, 3 putout," you'll know it means that the shortstop (6) threw the ball to the second baseman (4), who touched his base and then threw to the first baseman (3), making the double play.

Many methods and scoring styles are used to track the plays. They are given letters or symbols such as the following:

K — strikeout

Ks — strikeout, swinging

Kc — strikeout, called

BB — base-on-balls (walk)

IW — intentional walk

Bk — balk

SF — sacrifice fly

Sac — sacrifice bunt

E — on base through an error

HP — hit by pitch

FC — fielder's choice

PB — passed ball

FO — force-out

SB — stolen base

CS — caught stealing

S — single

D — double

T — triple

HR — home run

B — bunt

DP — double play

F — fly hit

FB — foul ball

LF — left field

RF — right field

CF — center field

WP — wild pitch

This sample scoring card shows how each at-bat is accounted for in every inning. The play and fielders' positions, when appropriate, are included.

DATE: May 20   TEAM: Donlands Dairy

PLAYER	Pos.#	1	2	3	4	5	6	7	8	9	10	11	AB	R	H	RBI	SO
AL	7	7 SB /HP	K		6-4 /5-1F	4-3			◆ D-RF	K			5	1	2	0	2
BOB	4	6-3	⑤	Ks	DP 6-4-3		7 WP /5-CF		7 /5-CF				5	0	2	1	0
CHUCK	6	/BB		◆ HR-CF	7 BB		Kc		② FB				3	0	0	0	2
DAVE	3	③ FB	⑨	F-3 5-SS	③ FB		6-3		⑨				5	1	2	2	0
EARL	8		7 BB	7 SB /E-5		◆ T-CF	4-3	7 D-CF	/BB	/BB			4	0	1	0	0
FRANK	9		Ks	7 SB /E-5		/HP		4-3	Ks	6-4 /5-CF			4	1	2	2	1
GORD	2		7 /S-B	4-3		SF-9		⑧		DP 6-4-3			4	0	1	0	1
HERB	5		/S-1F	/BB		Ks		5-3		/BB			3	0	1	1	0
IKE	1			⑤ F									4	0	1	0	1
TOTALS		RUNS 0	0	1	0	0	0	0	1	1			37	3	12	3	7
		HITS 0	2	2	2	1	1	1	2	1							

The sample scorecard shown here indicates how your neighborhood team performed. Let's look at the third inning:

Chuck (shortstop) struck out swinging.
Dave (first base) hit a home run to center field.

125

Earl (center field) singled to shortstop; he ran to third on an error by the third baseman, who overthrew to first attempting to get the batter/runner out.

Frank (right field) got to first on a fielding error by the third baseman, then stole second base.

Gord (catcher) grounded out to second base.

Herb (third base) walked.

Ike (pitcher) out on hit to third base.

The inning left your team with 1 run on 2 hits. Although 7 batters came to the plate, the walk does not count as an at-bat, leaving your team with an official 6 at-bats. They left the bases loaded.

Create your own scoring card by tracing the one shown here and writing in the names of the players according to their spot in the batting order. Enter their position number alongside. As each person comes to bat, use the correct symbol to show what happened.

Indicate an unassisted "out" by circling the fielder's number. Show a baserunner's progress by drawing that part of the diamond shape he moves along. Indicate where the hits went: S-LF = single hit to left field; HR-CF = home run over center field. Then add each player's total of batting and fielding plays across from his name. Add the team totals at the bottom of the page.

By the end of the game, you will have all the information that the next day's newspaper will publish, and you can use that to check your own scoring.

An error is judged by the Official Scorer as an unsuccessful play that should have been accomplished. For instance, a flyball is hit to the rightfielder, who loses his concentration and fumbles the ball, letting the batter get on base. The Official Scorer may decide that the play was not exceptionally difficult to make and call this a fielder's error. The batter does not get credit for a hit, but it is an at-bat. Likewise, the pitcher will not be penalized by an earned run if that batter makes it around to score during the inning.

The National
Baseball Hall of
Fame and Museum

Cooperstown, New York, opened the doors of the National Baseball Hall of Fame and Museum on June 12, 1939. The museum showcases the sport's legendary players and artifacts and provides a scholarly record of the game's development. Visitors can see early team line-up cards and scoring charts. Changes in equipment design over the years show up in a parade of styles: the tiny leather mitts resembling golf gloves; the baggy flannel uniforms worn until 1959; the balls and bats used by great players.

To be given membership in the Hall of Fame is to receive baseball's highest honor. It is awarded to players and individuals for their great accomplishments in the sport. Names are suggested and voted on by members of the Baseball Writers' Association and a committee under the authority of the Baseball Commissioner. To be nominated, a player must have been retired for at least five years. A candidate must receive at least 75 percent of the total votes to be inducted into the Hall of Fame.

The First Players Elected to the Hall of Fame:
George Herman "Babe" Ruth — "The Sultan of Swat" knocked 60 home runs in 151 games, a record that still stands today. That 1927 feat topped his earlier 1921 record, when he hit 59 homers. The Babe's boisterous displays on and off the field remain legendary.

Ty Cobb — Known for his fierce and aggressive style, "The Georgia Peach" supposedly sharpened his cleats to terrify the basemen on his spikes-up slides. His records for most career hits and stolen bases stood for more than 50 years.

Honus Wagner — "The Flying Dutchman" was also known as "The Greatest Shortstop — Ever." Wagner used his large hands and stocky body to block hits from leaving the infield. He led the National League for eight years for stolen bases, and between 1900 and 1911 won eight batting titles. For 17 consecutive years, Wagner hit over .300, still the current National League record!

Walter Johnson — "The Big Train" threw fastballs so hard that batters claimed only to be able to hear them crossing the plate. His career total of 3,508 strikeouts was unbeaten for nearly 50 years. His record of 113 shutouts still stands.

Christy Mathewson — "Big Six," nicknamed for his height, Mathewson was a popular sports hero in the early decades. Four times he pitched more than 30 winning games in a season — an unrivaled National League record. Mathewson threw with amazing control, even mastering the screwball. One season he pitched 306 innings with such accuracy he walked only 21 batters.

BASEBALL CARDS

Collecting and trading baseball cards was once a fun hobby during recess breaks in the schoolyard. Today, buying and dealing sports cards has become a full-time profession for a lot of people. That's because those colorful cardboard cards could be worth anywhere from hundreds to many thousands of dollars!

Baseball cards have been around since 1887. Dealers rate them from being in poor condition — torn, damaged, seriously creased or marked with pen or pencil — to mint condition, meaning they look brand-new. The age and the condition of a baseball card has a lot to do with its price.

Mistakes by manufacturers have started another craze for collectors: cards printed with errors. Sometimes artwork, design and printing problems on a particular card are not spotted until the card is already circulating. The manufacturer may end the circulation and reissue that card in a corrected version. The few cards with errors are hard to find and so they become valuable.

In the early 1900s, a company called the American Tobacco Trust was printing baseball cards to give away in cigarette packages. Honus Wagner — the Flying Dutchman — appeared in the T-206 series between 1909 and 1910. But Wagner hated smoking or chewing tobacco, and he threatened to sue the American Tobacco Trust unless they stopped printing his card. They obeyed, before very many of Wagner's cards were distributed. Today, fewer than seven of those cards are known to exist. Once given away free, this rarest of all sports cards is now the most expensive. One such card in excellent condition sold for $451,000 U.S. to pro sports team owner Bruce McNall and hockey star Wayne Gretzky. (Gretzky knows the value of sports cards from personal experience: his own rookie card is now worth hundreds of dollars!)

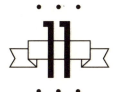

Extra Innings

EARLY HITS

What magic formula creates a major league baseball player? If the experiences of several Toronto Blue Jays are any indication, the trick is to start young — and to have fun with the family.

As a youngster, catcher Pat Borders, MVP (Most Valuable Player) of the 1992 World Series, never used a batting tee.

"My dad threw to me a lot. I hit a baseball more or less every day for years. I enjoyed it and had a lot of fun practising with my dad. No question about it, he was the biggest influence on me for learning the game."

When his father took Pat to Riverfront Stadium to see his local heroes, the Cincinnati Reds, the 8-year-old realized the sport was more than just something played in the backyard. After the family moved to Florida a few years later, an unexpected baseball opportunity arose.

"I lived down here as a kid, 15 or 20 minutes from a park. And on Saturdays and Sundays every once in a while, I'd go to a game with my dad, and I'd chase after the foul balls. I didn't really watch the games a whole lot. I was more interested in chasing after the foul balls and then practising with them afterward!"

Those errant baseballs plucked from the seats and behind the outfield fences let the future Blue Jays' backstop get the feel of the real thing. But Borders confesses he wasn't a superstar then.

"My skills didn't really advance much better than the other high school players. I was maybe a little better, but not that much. They were pretty comparable."

He credits his parents for giving him the extra edge to be where he is today.

"The family supports you and helps you out with baseball, otherwise it makes it much harder. Your father and mother have got to be interested in it. And they're going to have to help from time to time to make you progress to this level."

The Jays' hot-hitting first baseman, John Olerud, had the best batting average of all players in the majors in 1993. Part of the reason has to be the early start he made as a hitter; that evidence is preserved on film.

"We had home movies where I'd be taking batting practice with one of those whiffle ball bats and my dad would be throwing a little plastic block. I'd hit the block and then pretend I'd be running around the bases. That's probably the first memory that really sticks out."

The fact that his father played minor league baseball for several years gave the youngster a strong desire to take up the game. However, even a future "infield anchor" had limitations to endure.

"We lived right across the street from a playing field and they had Little League tryouts going on. I wanted to join but I couldn't because I was 7 and you had to be 8 to play in that league. That was kind of torture for me, watching everybody playing baseball and me not being able to play."

Temporarily excluded from that experience, Olerud junior relied upon his father to help him sharpen up on the fundamentals.

"Baseball for me early on was always something my dad and I did for fun.

"Whenever we'd have some free time we'd play, and just make a game out of everything, like seeing how many ground balls you could field. It was a lot of fun."

When the time came to join a team, Olerud's father pitched in by helping to coach. The man's enthusiasm for turning practice into playtime made a lasting impression on his son.

"I was fortunate that he really got involved in baseball. The other coaches in high school, they were well-organized. They'd do some instructing, but I think I got most of my instruction from my dad."

In baseball, as with any sport or profession, he adds, "the most important thing is having fun."

John Olerud tied Ted Williams?

Not for the battle of hitting .400, but in drawing the most intentional walks. Fearful pitchers gave Olerud free passage to first base 33 times in 1993, tying Ted Williams's 1957 American League record.

For pitcher Dave Stewart, MVP of the 1993 American League Championship Series, his first look at "The Boys of Summer" came when his father took him to Candlestick Park in San Francisco.

"My dad used to take me out to watch the Giants originally, and as I got older we started to watch the Athletics when they moved to Oakland."

The West Coast rivalry between 'Frisco and Los Angeles worked its way into the Stewart family home.

"With my brother, we started out playing in the backyard. We'd play a game of strike-out. That's my earliest memory. My brother was always the Giants and I was always the Dodgers."

(By coincidence years later, Dave Stewart was drafted by the L.A. Dodgers.)

A turning point for the youngster came when he had an encounter with a future Hall of Famer.

"Reggie Jackson was the first professional player I ever met and who took notice. He helped me in the younger years by leaving me tickets into the game and really just taking time to get to know me as a kid, and that was a big plus.

"I was 13 at the time, just a kid at the ballpark. He took a liking to me and we've gotten along together ever since."

That togetherness came full circle when Stewart himself turned pro and met Jackson on the field. "I've played with him and against him. I've been on both ends."

Now that he himself is a father, Dave Stewart is sometimes asked for his suggestions by other parents and teachers on how to deal with kids going through a crisis stage.

"As a parent, it's always tough to know whether you have the rope too tight or whether the rope is too loose.

"We've all been blessed to be able to see things usually before they happen and if you follow the guidelines of being a parent, it means to make your kids aware, to make them knowledgable. You can't hold their hands through life. Just do the best as a parent."

1993 was the first time in 100 years that three players from the same team finished 1-2-3 at the top of the league for best Batting Average: John Olerud (.363), Paul Molitor (.332) and Roberto Alomar (.326)

The path taken by Roberto Alomar, Golden Glove winner and all-star second baseman, to his choice of career seemed predestined: he grew up around the clubhouse where his father, Sandy Alomar, was a major leaguer. Brother Sandy Jr. is a catcher with the Cleveland Indians.

"Baseball was always a part of my life since I was born. I always wanted to be a baseball player and nothing else, because my dad was one, too. And the dream of any kid is to follow in his dad's footsteps, so that's what I did."

He shrugged off any suggestion about being pressured to take up the sport. "It's something that God gave me: the ability to play that game. If I didn't have it to play baseball, I'd be doing something else, but He gave me that ability. And watching my dad play for 15 years in the big leagues — why not?"

The apprenticeship began in a way that most young-sters can only dream about: helping keep the bats, balls and helmets organized in the dugout.

"I was a batboy on a few occasions. I'd put on a uniform and go hang around with the players, learn from them and have some fun... I never knew where it was going to end up. I wanted to play baseball, but you never know what can happen in life."

Growing up with an active older brother gave young Roberto opportunities to test himself, to try harder to keep up.

"We used to play basketball, volleyball, a lot of games. My brother was more into motorcycles, karate and other scary stuff. I wasn't into that. I was more into basketball and baseball, my two favorite sports. I used to run track, too, but if I had to make a choice it was basketball or baseball."

Now when he encounters brother Sandy crouched behind the plate or as a baserunner, their relationship is all business.

"This is a job. And I have to take care of my job. We're brothers off the field and on the field, but when we go out there we have to give 100 per cent and each take care of our jobs."

Alomar advises teenagers to keep themselves healthy and remain in school. Following a few basic rules paves the road to success in any field, he adds.

"Stay away from drugs and alcohol. Be a good student and you'll be okay."

Add to that his own personal motto for becoming a winner: "The bottom line is to go out there and work hard. Especially in life, where nothing's easy, either."

A Baseball Dictionary

ACE — a top pitcher

AT-BAT — a player in the batter's box who is waiting to hit; for scoring purposes, no at-bat is counted against a player when he is walked, hits a sacrifice or is struck by a pitch

BAG — a base

BALK — an illegal move made by the pitcher toward home plate or a base after he stands on the rubber and prepares to pitch while there are one or more baserunners; runners may advance one base

BALL — a pitch thrown out of the strike zone, at which the batter does not swing

BASE HIT — a ball put into play that lets a batter get on base safely

BASE-ON-BALLS — four pitches thrown outside of the strike zone and not swung at, which gives the batter free passage, or a "walk," to first base

BASES LOADED — runners occupy first, second and third bases

BATTER'S BOX — a rectangular area chalk-marked on the ground on either side of home plate; the batter must remain in it while being pitched to

BATTING AVERAGE (OR PERCENTAGE) — a batter's

number of hits divided by his official at-bat appearances

BATTING ORDER — the sequence of batters who come
to the plate

BULLPEN — an area beside the playing field where a
pitching squad practices

BUNT — a bat held steady and not swung, so that the
ball bounces off it into fair territory in the infield

CALLED GAME — a game stopped by the umpire,
usually because of bad weather

CAUGHT STEALING — occurs to a baserunner who is
trying to steal a base and gets tagged by a fielder
with the ball

CHANGE-OF-PACE — a slower pitch intended to
confuse the timing of the batter's swing

CHECK SWING — a half-swing that the batter holds
back or stops in mid-motion by not rolling his wrists
or letting the bat pass over the plate; the catcher will
appeal to a base umpire to call a strike if the bat is
swung too far

CLEAN-UP — the fourth player in the batting order
(usually the team's best hitter), who is expected to
hit and "clean up" the bases of any runners waiting
to come home

CLUTCH HITTER — a batter in a crucial point during
the game who successfully comes through with a hit

COUNT — the number of balls and strikes on a batter;
the count is always given by the balls first, strikes

second; for example, a count of two-and-one means two balls and one strike

CYCLE — when he hits a single, double, triple and home run in one game, a batter "hits the cycle"

DESIGNATED HITTER — a hitter who takes the place of the pitcher in the batting order throughout the game; not applicable to the National League

DIAMOND — the "diamond-shaped" infield area

DOUBLE — a hit that brings the batter to second base

DOUBLEHEADER — two games played in the same day, one right after the other

DOUBLE PLAY — two "outs" that occur as a result of the same fielding action

DUGOUT — the area in foul territory where players and coaches sit; these places have been "dug out" of the ground so that fans behind the benches have an unobstructed view

EARNED RUN — a run for which the pitcher is held accountable

EARNED RUN AVERAGE (ERA) — the number of runs a pitcher is responsible for allowing against his team over a nine-inning period; it does not include runs scored as a result of any fielding errors

ERROR — a mistake charged against a fielder for mishandling a play that lets a runner advance a base

EXTRA BASE HIT — a double, triple or homer

EXTRA INNINGS — additional innings played if the score is tied at the end of nine complete innings; the game continues until one team is in the lead at the end of a complete inning

FAIR BALL — a ball hit into legal play in fair territory

FAIR TERRITORY — the area between the first and third baselines, extending outward from home plate to the outfield fences

FIELDER'S CHOICE — the fielder must choose between possible "outs"; for example, he may throw out a runner coming into third and "allow" the batter to reach first safely

FLYBALL — a hit that goes directly from the bat into the air, without hitting the ground

FORCE PLAY — a play that results when a runner must move ahead to the next base because of a runner advancing behind him; the fielder with the ball needs only to touch the bag to force "out" the oncoming runner

FOUL BALL — a ball that is hit into foul territory

FOUL TERRITORY — the area to the right of first base and to the left of third base, extending outward from home plate to the outfield fences

FRAME — slang term for an inning

FUNGO — a ball tossed up and hit by the same person to other players for fielding practice

GRAND SLAM — a home run while runners occupy all three bases

GROUNDER — a ball that is hit off the bat and bounces along the field

HIT — a ball put safely into play by the batter which gets him on base

HIT-AND-RUN — a tactic ordered by the coach; a runner starts for the next base as the pitcher begins his delivery and the batter tries to hit whatever ball is thrown

HIT-BY-PITCH — a batter struck by the ball while standing in his batter's box; he automatically goes to first base

HOME RUN — a hit allowing the batter to run around all three bases and return to home safely; nearly all home runs are balls hit beyond the outfield fences in fair territory, but some "inside-the-park" home runs occur as a result of fielding mishaps

HOT BOX — the area between two bases in which a runner is chased during a rundown

HOT CORNER — third base, so-called for all the blistering hits that come here

INFIELD — the area bordered by home plate, first base, second base and third base

INNING — the period of a game in which each team has a turn at bat; the visiting team bats first and the home team completes the inning

INTENTIONAL WALK — on a coach's instructions for game strategy, the pitcher throws four balls far outside of the strike zone to place the runner on base

KEYSTONE — second base, so-called because a runner who gets here is in a key scoring position

NO-HITTER — a game in which a pitcher completes nine innings with no batters getting a hit

ON-DECK — the next batter waiting to come to the plate

OUT — a batter or runner who is retired from play by the defensive team during his own team's inning at bat

PASSED BALL — failure by the catcher to stop a pitch that gets away from him and that lets a runner advance a base

PERCENTAGE — see BATTING AVERAGE

PERFECT GAME — a game in which a pitcher faces 27 batters (three per inning for nine innings) and gets 27 consecutive outs with no batters getting on base through walks, errors or hit-by-pitches

PICK-OFF PLAY — a play in which a baseman catches the ball from another player to touch a runner who is off his base

PINCH HITTER — a new batter who replaces another player in the batting line-up; the substituted player cannot come back into the game

PINCH RUNNER — a baserunner who replaces a team member already on base; the substituted player cannot come back into the game

PITCHER'S RUBBER — a block, 24 inches long and 6 inches wide, embedded in the center of the pitcher's mound, on which the pitcher must keep one foot during his delivery

POP-FLY — a high but weak hit, easily caught

RELIEF PITCHER — a pitcher brought in during the game to replace another pitcher

RUNDOWN PLAY — a play in which a runner is trapped on the basepaths as the fielders throw the ball back and forth as they give chase to tag him "out"

RUNS BATTED IN (RBI) — a statistic that credits a batter for getting one or more runners to home plate on a hit

SACRIFICE — a bunt that results in the batter getting "out" but that safely advances a runner

SACRIFICE FLY — a flyball that is caught but allows the runner at third to tag up and score on

SAFE — reaching a base before the ball is caught there

SAVE — the scoring credit a relief pitcher receives for successfully finishing the game and holding the lead

SEVENTH-INNING STRETCH — a baseball ritual that involves the fans standing up to stretch in the middle of the seventh inning to give the home team good luck

SHUTOUT — a game in which one team does not score a runner at home plate

SINGLE — a hit that advances the batter to first base

SLUGGING PERCENTAGE — the total number of bases a player achieves on a hit, divided by the total number of at-bats

SQUEEZE PLAY — a play in which a runner on third base starts for home plate as the pitcher delivers the ball; the batter bunts and the runner "squeezes" in to score

STOLEN BASE — achieved when a player advances safely to the next base without the assistance of a base hit, walk or error

STRIKE — a pitch in the strike zone that the batter doesn't put into play

STRIKE ZONE — the area above home plate that is between the batter's armpits and the top of his knees while in his normal standing posture

SWITCH HITTER — a batter who can hit effectively from either the left or right side of the plate

TAG — a fielder holding the ball touches a runner who is off-base to make an "out"

TAG-UP — a runner must touch his base after a flyball is caught before attempting to race onto the next base

TRIPLE — a hit that brings the batter safely to third base

WILD PITCH — an out-of-control throw made by the pitcher that the catcher has no chance of stopping; baserunners can attempt to advance as many bases as possible

WIN/LOSS PERCENTAGE — a team statistic; the total number of wins divided by the total number of games played

Notable Statistics

BASEBALL'S GREATEST PITCHERS

FOR A SINGLE SEASON:

HIGHEST WINNING PERCENTAGE   W/L   Pct.
- Roy Face, Pittsburgh Pirates (1959)   18–1   .947

MOST WINS   W
- Jack Chesbro, New York Yankees (1904)   41

MOST STRIKEOUTS   SO
- Nolan Ryan, California Angels (1973)   383

MOST SHUTOUTS   ShO
- Grover Alexander, Philadelphia
  Phillies (1916)   16

LOWEST EARNED RUN AVERAGE   ERA
- Dutch Leonard, Boston Red Sox (1914)   0.96

FOR ALL-TIME:

HIGHEST WINNING PERCENTAGE   W/L   Pct.
- Cy Young   511–313   .620

MOST WINS (since 1900)   W
- Walter Johnson   416

MOST STRIKEOUTS (to '93)   SO
• Nolan Ryan   5,714
MOST SHUTOUTS   ShO
• Walter Johnson   113
MOST NO-HITTERS (to '92)   Games
• Nolan Ryan   7

BASEBALL'S HITTING LEADERS

FOR A SINGLE SEASON:

HIGHEST BATTING AVERAGE   Avg.
• Rogers Hornsby, St. Louis Browns (1924)   .424

MOST BASE HITS   H
• George Sisler, St. Louis Browns (1920)   257

MOST HOME RUNS   HR
• Roger Maris, New York Yankees (1961)   61

MOST TOTAL BASES   TBs
• Babe Ruth, New York Yankees (1921)   457

MOST RUNS BATTED IN   RBIs
• Hack Wilson, Chicago Cubs (1930)   190

LONGEST CONSECUTIVE-GAME
HITTING STREAK   Games
• Joe DiMaggio, New York Yankees (1941)   56

FOR ALL-TIME:

HIGHEST BATTING AVERAGE | Avg.
• Ty Cobb | .366

MOST BASE HITS | H
• Pete Rose | 4,256

MOST HOME RUNS | HR
• Hank Aaron | 755

MOST TOTAL BASES | TBs
• Hank Aaron | 6,856

MOST RUNS BATTED IN | RBIs
• Hank Aaron | 2,297

LONGEST CONSECUTIVE-GAME
HITTING STREAK | Games
• Joe DiMaggio | 56

Baseball's Basic
Arithmetic

Teams

Win/Loss Percentage = $\dfrac{\text{total wins}}{\text{total wins + losses}}$

Games-behind-Leader =

$$\dfrac{\left(\begin{array}{c}\text{top team's wins minus} \\ \text{Team X's wins}\end{array}\right) + \left(\begin{array}{c}\text{Team X's losses minus} \\ \text{top team's losses}\end{array}\right)}{2}$$

Individuals

Batting Average =
(see p. 116)
$\dfrac{\text{total hits}}{\text{total at-bats}}$

Slugging Percentage =
(see p. 118)
$\dfrac{\text{total number of bases}}{\text{total at-bats}}$

Earned Run Average =
(see p. 119)
$\dfrac{\text{total earned runs x 9}}{\text{total innings pitched}}$

Fielding Percentage =
(see p. 122)
$\dfrac{\text{put outs + assists}}{\text{put outs + assists + errors}}$

Sports Books Ordering Information

Ask for any of the books listed below at your bookstore. Or to order direct from the publisher, call 1-800-447-BOOK (MasterCard or Visa), or send a check or money order for the books purchased (plus $4.00 shipping and handling for the first book ordered and 75¢ for each additional book) to Carol Publishing Group, 120 Enterprise Avenue, Dept. 1620, Secaucus, NJ 07094.

Settle-Your-Bet Sports Trivia Books
Questions, Answers (and Photos) Covering Every Professional Sport Team--Past & Present--From the Following Cities:

Boston Sports Quiz by Brenda Alesii & Daniel Locche; Paperback $9.95 (#51212)

Chicago Sports Quiz by Brenda Alesii & Daniel Locche; Paperback $9.95 (#51372)

Los Angeles Sports Quiz by Brenda Alesii & Daniel Locche; Paperback $10.95 (#51381)

New York Sports Quiz by Brenda Alesii & Daniel Locche; Paperback $10.95 (#51215)

Philadelphia Sports Quiz by Brenda Alesii & Daniel Locche; Paperback $9.95 (#51416)

The Ultimate Sports Trivia Book: The Official Bar Book of Runyon's Saloon by Jim Benagh & Tim Hays; Paperback $8.95 (#51273)

Washington/Baltimore Sports Quiz by Brenda Alesii & Daniel Locche; Paperback $10.95 (#51424)

Tennis Books

Love Match: Nelson vs. Navratilova by Sandra Faulkner w/Judy Nelson; Hardcover w/16 pages of photos. $19.95 (#72157)

World Tennis Magazine's Guide to the Best Tennis Resorts by Peter Coan w/Barry Stambler; Paperback $10.95 (#51272)

Boxing Books

The Autobiography of Jack Johnson: In the Ring and Out; Paperback, illustrated w/ photos throughout. $10.95 (#51358)

Boxing Babylon: Behind the Shadowy World of the Prize Ring by Nigel Collins; Hardcover, illustrated w/photos throughout. $18.95 (#51183)

Mike Tyson: Money, Myth & Betrayal by Monteith Illingworth; Hardcover w/8 pages of photos. $22.95 (#72079)

A Pictorial History of Boxing: Revised and Updated Edition by Sam Andre & Nat Fleischer, updated by Peter Arnold; *Illustrated w/ nearly 2000 photos & prints.* Oversized paperback. $19.95 (#51427)

Baseball Books

Dodgers: The First 100 Years by Stanley Cohen; Paperback, illustrated w/photos throughout. $4.50 (#62508)

Five O'Clock Lightning: Ruth, Gehrig, DiMaggio and the Glory Years of the New York Yankees by Tommy Henrich w/Bill Gilbert; Hardcover w/8 pages of photos. $19.95 (#72101)

Great Moments in Baseball: From the World Series of 1903 to the Modern Records of Nolan Ryan by Tom Seaver w/ Marty Appel; Paperback w/photos throughout. $12.95 (#51611)

Kids' Book of Baseball: Hitting, Fielding and the Rules of the Game by Godfrey Jordan; Paperback. $8.95 (#51620)

Say It Ain't So, Joe: The True Story of Shoeless Joe Jackson, revised edition by Donald Gropman; Paperback w/16 pages of photos. $10.95 (#51336)

The Worst Baseball Pitchers of All Time: Bad Luck, Bad Arms, Bad Teams, and Just Plain Bad by Alan S. Kaufman & James C. Kaufman; Paperback w/photos throughout. $9.95 (#51653)

Of Interest

The 100 Greatest Athletes of All Time: A Sports Editor's Personal Ranking by Bert Randolph Sugar; Hardcover, illustrated w/photos throughout. $24.95 (#51614)

The Golf Book of Days: Fascinating Golf Facts and Stories for Every Day of the Year by Robert McCord; Hardcover $18.95 (#72292)

(Prices subject to change; books subject to availability)